SOUL WORK

SOUL WORK

Confessions of a
Part-Time
Monk

RANDY HARRIS

LEAFWOOD
PUBLISHERS

SOUL WORK
CONFESSIONS OF A PART-TIME MONK

Copyright 2011 by Randy Harris

ISBN 978-0-89112-271-2
LCCN 2011010663

Printed in the United States of America

Scripture quotations, unless otherwise noted, are from The Holy Bible, New International Version. Copyright 1984, International Bible Society. Used by permission of Zondervan Publishers.

LIBRARY OF CONGRESS CATALOGING-IN-PUBLICATION DATA
Harris, Randy, 1958-
 Soul work : confessions of a part-time monk / Randy Harris.
    p. cm.
 ISBN 978-0-89112-272-2
 1. Spiritual life--Christianity. I. Title.
 BV4501.3.H367 2011
 248.4--dc22

                                                                    2011010663

Cover design by Marc Whitaker, MTW Design
Interior text design by Sandy Armstrong

Leafwood Publishers
1626 Campus Court
Abilene, Texas 79601
1-877-816-4455 toll free

For current information about all Leafwood titles, visit our Web site:
www.leafwoodpublishers.com

12 13 14 15 16 / 7 6 5 4 3 2

To the TXA monk warriors
who pursue the dangerous way of prayer

CONTENTS

INTRODUCTION

This is a book about the quest for sanity in a crazy world. Over the last dozen years this search has taken me into the presence of Carmelite hermits, Trappist monks, Celtic Christians, Franciscan monks, the Ignatian exercises, and a remarkable array of Christian mystics who have served as tour guides into the world of the Spirit. While that quest is hardly over, I have discovered what life can be in those moments when you embrace the ultimate reality of God's love in Jesus Christ and let go of the desperate striving that marks so much of contemporary life. I have tried crazy and I have tried sane and I like sane better. I often return to Whittier's glorious hymn lyrics:

> Drop Thy still dews of quietness,
> Till all our strivings cease;
> Take from our souls the strain and stress,
> And let our ordered lives confess
> The beauty of Thy peace.

It probably goes without saying (though I feel I need to say it) that I have theological disagreements with all the mystics who have taught me. I did not go to the desert to fine-tune my theological constructs. I went there to learn to pray and found kind, generous, expert guides.

Most Christians will not get to make the journey in the same way I have been blessed to do so due to the constraints of jobs, families, and other responsibilities—or perhaps due to the fear of the strange (a fear I know well!). So I am sharing my own journey in the hope that other seekers will be encouraged to find their personal path into a deeper relationship with God.

I must say that sharing one's personal spiritual journey is frightening in a way that sharing one's theology is not. It is too easy to leave the impression that I know more than I do or that my life is lived better than the reality. Years ago, in Hans Küng's book, *On Being a Christian*, he said he wrote the book, not because he thought he was a particularly good Christian, but because he thought a Christian was a particularly good thing to be. I want to echo that sentiment; I wrote this book not because I think I am a particularly good pray-er but because I think a pray-er is a particularly good thing to be.

And finally, as you begin this book I must issue the strongest possible warning: this quest for the depths of relationship with God is not about looking for the next experiential high or mystical encounter. It is about creating the space for God to do the work of making us radical Jesus followers. It is about how we live day to day. As Whittier says,

> In simple trust like theirs who heard
> Beside the Syrian sea
> The gracious calling of the Lord,
> Let us, like them, without a word
> Rise up and follow Thee.
>
> Amen!

Chapter 1

PRAYING WITH THE HERMITS

Over thirteen years ago the book *Experiencing God* by Henry Blackaby came out. Now, millions of copies later, what I learned most from the reception of that book was that people have a deep longing to experience God and when they got together with other people who had that same deep longing some wonderful things happened. One of the things that we've got to get over is being afraid of experience, because life in God was meant to be experienced. These are not facts to be believed, this is a life to be lived. Experience is not a dirty word. It's written on every line that Paul ever wrote. This is about living the life of the Holy Spirit.

Some of us have a concept of religious experience so narrow that when we think about having a religious experience what we envision is enthusiastic worship. We sing songs that move us, we work up some enthusiasm, and we have an emotional experience—and that becomes what we envision when we think about religious experience.

I want to take you down a completely different road and invite you to an experience of God that's something other than enthusiasm. This will be much like taking a long road trip with a really good friend. I want you to think about two different kinds of trips. First, think about the kind of trip that my father always took us on. Traveling with my father was very similar to a military death march. You would put gas in the car before you left. You would stop again when the gas tank was almost empty. Now how many of you travel that way? I am glad to say that my father has now reached the age where he has to stop whether he needs gas or not. Serves him right, I think. On that kind of trip the only thing that matters is the destination. What we're trying to do is simply get somewhere.

Now think about another kind of trip. Think about making a road trip with your buddies. Do you remember one of those trips? Half the time, when you take a road trip with your buddies, you never get there—but it doesn't matter. It's not the destination. It's the trip. Now with the Christian life, the destination does matter, to be sure; but the trip itself is the fun. Consider the Christian journey: God deeply and infinitely loves you and wants to spend time with you and he doesn't particularly always want you to be trying to get something out of him when you do.

I want to push the notion of the title of a book I read some time ago called *Wasting Time with God*. Is that a great title or what? This is about spending time with God and not particularly trying to get anything done while you're there. This is just walking and talking and becoming intimate with the one we say we love, and that becomes the whole point of life. It becomes the ground out of which all the rest of our ministry grows.

Experiencing Desperation

Let me start to put the first brick in the wall. Do you find prayer the least bit appealing? Sometimes we experience prayer as mainly a burden. Wouldn't it be nice every once in a while to experience prayer as a vacation? Going off and spending an hour walking and talking with the one I love, just spending time with God. It's like an hour's vacation every day. But often the ground out of which prayer grows is desperation. Everybody's prayed this kind of prayer, right? You get to that point where you realize that you're in trouble, that you're totally out of control. There's nothing like that to lead you to prayer.

For instance, have you ever prayed the following desperate prayer? "Gas station, gas station, gas station!" The problem is we do not realize our everyday desperation. There are moments when we experience being out of control and not having a handle on things, but through great portions of our life we think we're doing right well. One of the reasons I think we struggle with prayer so much is that we think we need it so little. We're not desperate people. We are, for the most part, affluent, well adjusted, happy, and don't feel much sense of not being in control of our lives. Not only are we in control of our lives, we're in control of a good many other people's lives too and that feels pretty good. And so we don't feel the need to pray.

So I think the first step toward living an intimate life with God is to realize our own desperation, and that desperation comes largely by developing some sense of God's holiness. As long as we're looking at our own lives compared to the mess that others have made of theirs, then we can feel pretty good about life and may not feel any great need. But if at some point we start to see ourselves against God's infinite holiness, we may truly begin to feel desperation.

Now this is hard to pull off because we haven't talked about holiness in a serious way for quite a long time now. We've been so intent on becoming close friends with Jesus that the holiness of God hasn't had much room at the table. That probably needs to change. We could look at a few passages. I suspect the one that you'd be most familiar with is Isaiah 6. Here Isaiah experiences this great vision of God where he says, "I saw him high and lifted up and the train of his robe filled the temple . . . ." Now that's pretty big. The train of his robe filled the temple! Are you kidding me? This is not really like a wedding train. The train, I guess, would be the hem of the robe and can you imagine the hem of the robe filling the temple? This huge, majestic figure arises and then there's these angelic beings flying around with six wings. With two wings they fly, with two they cover their faces, and with two they cover their feet (which is almost surely a euphemism meaning genitals, a sign of impotence). Listen to what the passage says: "When these angelic beings fly around the almighty God what they do is cower before him. They don't stand in awe. They run for cover."

Think about the Mount Sinai experience in the Old Testament. We blithely pray that we want to see God's presence, but in the Old Testament, when people see God's presence they never ask for a second dose. When almighty God comes off that mountain and appears to the Israelites, they tell Moses, "Don't you ever let him do that again. You let him speak to you and then you speak to us, but tell God never to speak to us again unless we die."

But God still sits on the throne. And when we see that God we do what Isaiah did—we say, "Woe is me. I am undone. I am a man of unclean lips and I dwell in the midst of a people of unclean lips for my eyes have seen the Lord." Then we can pray. I believe from my own experience, from talking to a few others, and from reading a book or two, that if we get serious about walking with God, the initial part of that experience is a bit painful. Because what has to happen for that to be an authentic walk is we have to lose the illusions we have about ourselves and our self-sufficiency and our goodness and our competence. All of those just get burned away when you stand before the holy God.

When I lived in New York, I once tried golf evangelism. This turned out to be poor golf and worse evangelism. But I tried. I was playing a little guy who was on the golf team and we start to play and he's three shots ahead, six shots ahead, nine shots ahead, then twelve shots ahead. Who cares? So we get to about the fifteenth hole and I said, "Tommy, have you ever read the novels of Dostoevsky?" He said, "No." I say, "I have. In fact, that's what I was doing when you were practicing golf. Just wanted you to know that while you were playing golf, I was getting an education. Thought I'd point that out. Go ahead, hit now."

That's what we do. I never come to the full realization of my situation with God as long as I'm looking at you, because I can always find some area of life in which I'm superior to you. I might have to look for a while. But if you start to commune with the living God, everything else disappears. It's just you and God, and it's pretty hard to find any place to run and hide. Then you come to see your-self as you really are. "Woe is me, I am undone." Our tendency at that point is to run away because who needs this? It can be such a painful experience that it just scares us away. We'll go back to a kind of praying where we give God the laundry list and ask him to bless all those things. That's the kind of prayer relationship we'll have because I can pray all day like that and never have to think about me. I never have to deal with my situation before God.

Spending Time with One Who Loves Us

I want to encourage you to stay around long enough with God so you will have this extraordinary experience. The God who reveals is the God who heals and he loves you just the way you are. Now here's our problem. We all know that. I know that. I love to teach the book of Romans and I can talk about salvation by grace in a way that will make people weep. The question is do we *experience* that? Do we understand what it means to walk through life with God knowing that we have no righteousness of our own to claim, but that God loves us just the way we are. Do we *experience* that? Because that makes all the difference in the world. It means we're not just living on the inside of our head, but really experiencing the walk with the living God.

How many of you took one year of a foreign language but never took a second year? How many of you are fluent in a second language? I'm still working on one language. English comes a little harder when you're from Arkansas. I want to remind you what the first year of taking a language is like—for those of you who need the unhappy reminder. It is like taking your hand, putting it on the table, getting a very heavy hammer, and hitting each finger repeatedly. It's absolutely miserable. The only thing comparable to it is the beginning stages of learning a musical instrument or (what's worse) being in the house with someone who is. I lived with some people in New York for a time. She was trying to learn to play the piano. If I ever hear "Für Elise" again it will be too soon. Du du du du du du da. It was awful.

What often happens is we take the first year of a language then we quit studying it. We experience all the pain but never experience the joy of being able to speak another language. Or we take one year of lessons to learn a musical instrument. We experience all the pain but we never experience the real joy of being able to make any decent music. I was a sax player. I know all about that. The saxophone doesn't sound good unless you play it right. I can just hear my parents now. Is the car horn going off? No, that's Randy. He's practicing.

But if you're willing to abide long enough with God as he reveals the secrets of your heart, you'll discover that he'll heal you and that he loves you just the way you are and that he's calling you into relationship with him that he deeply and infinitely wants. Of all the creatures in the universe, he's chosen you by name to join him on a road trip. What a way to live!

• The One Who Takes Care of Everything

The great thing about this is that it's like going on a road trip with the person who has the ability to take care of everything. Have you ever been in a situation in a foreign country where you felt totally out of control and at someone else's mercy? My worst experience of that was my trip to Nigeria. I found it a difficult country to negotiate. I didn't know what was going on there. They didn't give me very much information before I went. Lots of people are wearing uniforms of various types and you don't know who the good guys are and who the bad guys are. I quickly learned to assume that they're all bad guys. But someone there took care of me. He took me where I needed to go and even began to help me with my teaching.

I was there to teach theology, and guess what the two biggest theological topics in the country were at the time? Number one was syncretism. That is, how much of traditional African religion can you keep and be a Christian? The other was polygamy. And I know you're going to find this hard to believe, but nothing in my theological training had prepared me for either topic. Back in my churches at home, multiple wives were not a problem. I was just trying to get men to keep the one they had.

One day I put on Nigerian dress to go out to preach and I came down the stairs and one of the Nigerians says, "Oh, now he's a Nigerian." And I thought, "Boy, I wish." I wish you could dress up and be able to understand and think like a Nigerian, but it doesn't work that way. I was totally at the mercy of the people who were helping me.

Here's what I want you to understand. When you start to walk with God he's got everything under control and you don't have to worry about having your act all together because he's got his together and just by being around he's going to help you. If you're willing to walk and talk and spend time with God, he'll start to remake your life even when you don't know what's going on. Most of us have had that experience, right? We have had the experience of having someone change who we are simply by being with us. That's what God wants. He wants to remake you and bring you along and help you be everything you were created to be. And he can do that if you just spend some time with him.

But it all starts with this poverty of spirit and being willing to realize that we're not all that competent. We're not all that together. We're not all that perfect. But being willing to experience the God who loves us anyway will transform us.

Forty Days with the Hermits

Let me tell you about an important part of my walk with God. It began when I heard of Lebh Shomea, a house of prayer, basically a hermits' community. I know it's a bit of a problem to speak of a hermits' *community*. But they've got to live somewhere. So these three hermits make up the core community and you can go there to pray anytime you desire. But they have one program. It's called a forty-day desert experience. It's down in south Texas. It's desert. You go there and spend forty days in contemplative prayer. You get some instruction in St. John of the Cross and Thomas Merton and folks like that, and then you spend about six hours a day just praying.

My first couple of weeks there were quite unpleasant. It wasn't just because of the heat and the food and tedium, although there was that. It was rather due to what I discovered when I got quiet before God. When I no longer had words to justify or rationalize myself and I had nobody to compare myself to and I was alone with God, what happened is that all the crud in my life came rushing to the surface—which I didn't particularly like. All the woundedness. All the sin. All the pain.

My question is, "How can a person who can talk about salvation by grace from Romans in a way that will make people weep understand it so little?" What I discovered is the monastic way—to just take a road trip with God. Just spend time with God and look at yourself and look at God. If you do that, he will give to your heart what you have in your head.

The point here is not to go out and get some special revelation from God that will tell you what you're supposed to do tomorrow. God may do that for you. He hasn't done that for me. I sometimes wish that he would! I'm not against it. I'd like to get in on it. But what I'm pretty sure of is, whether that happens or not, if you are willing to invest time with God, what he will do is teach you the gospel. Not with the head but with the heart.

And if you can ever let go of being the smartest kid in school, or being the child whom nobody loved, or being the failure—if you can give up all those identities that our woundedness and our sins give to us—what you're left with is a God who loves you because he created you and wants to spend time with you. Wow, that is liberating! With that you'll walk through the world in a completely different way. If that's all you got out of forty days in the desert, I'd say that was a pretty good investment, wouldn't you?

Now my problem is this: I can talk about that but there's a real sense in which I cannot give it to you. Some of you are longing for that, and even though it's not mine to give, I deeply believe it's available to you. God hasn't done anything for me he won't do for you. If we take this road of spending time with God and quit pushing our agenda and let him have his, I think he'll do that for you. Because he's infinitely loving and he wants more than anything else to be in a relationship with you that isn't impaired by your own absurd sense of competence. Begin to give that up and then you can walk with God.

This poverty of spirit or humility will be worked out in the world in certain ways. The Benedictine monks say that what happens is, when you look around at other people, you see the Christ. I want you to think about how that's different from what we often talk about, which is *being* the Christ. We want to be the Christ in people's midst. What would happen if, when you looked around at all the people you encounter, what you did is to *see* Christ? All of a sudden, arrogance and self-sufficiency and all that stuff just disappear. It's impossible to take a position of superiority with any person when you see in them the Christ. Rather, you start to engage in a kind of service to them that cannot be driven by duty, but is driven by seeing the Christ. Then humility or poverty of spirit becomes not just a theory but something we live out in life and practice.

Life in Community

One of the things I'm going to try to get you to see, and I'm passionate about this, is that time alone with God and the spirituality of the desert does not separate you from community. It opens you up to new community. Because now you have a better understanding of who you are and who God is and how he cares about that other person and how he cares about you. You can relate to that person in a way you never could have before.

One of the reasons we do so badly with people is that we spend so much time with them. Richard Foster says that sometimes we need to fast from people because we eat too many of them. They give us indigestion. Most of us have that experience. The worst mistakes I made in ministry happened when I was fatigued. And we do that. We make mistakes. There have been times when I'd say to the church staff, "Look, we can't make any decisions today, because it's obvious everybody's too tired here to think. We need to back up and spend some time with God."

One of the great things about being at Lebh Shomea was that there was nothing to do. So when I would go out in the desert to pray there was no hurry to get back, because when I got back there was nothing to do. And in the evenings I would often find myself rocking on the porch. It was like Andy Griffith. And I would find myself thinking in Andy Griffith-like ways. I would be rocking and thinking to myself, "I think I might go get a drink. Yeah, maybe I'll go get a drink. No, I think I'll rock here a few more minutes and then I'll think again about maybe going to get a drink."

I mean, for a guy who's been in the fast-paced way of life for a while, this came as a revelation. I began to develop some appreciation for those conversations. Trying to decide whether to go down to the drugstore and get an ice cream bar or just sit. That's tough. When you build a bit of that into your life—rocking on the porch with God—it will not take away from your ministry. It's just going to help you minister better.

We have the notion that the contemplative life is going to lead us away from the hurly burly of life. I think it's just the opposite. I think it gives you some leverage on it and some perspective on it. It keeps us from being so nutty.

In the next chapter, I'm going to talk about the word "amen," which is much more loaded than you think. "Amen" is about a declaration of total surrender to God. It's like the Lipton tea commercials. The old ones. You remember those? Where the guy would fall back in the water. That's what "amen" does. It looks at God's grace and says, "Okay, here I go," and falls back into the water.

Then in the next chapter, I'm going to tell you what it's like to be a monk who doesn't have a monastery. That is, I want to talk about how to live a contemplative life in the midst of ministry in the world. Because most of us are not going to become hermits. Some people may be called to that. Most of us probably aren't. I want to talk about how you can start to incorporate that life into how you live.

CHAPTER TWO

LEARNING TOTAL SURRENDER FROM THE HERMITS

Let me tell you about a woman who is a Christian but whose husband isn't. Not only is he not a Christian, he is hostile to Christianity. He is verbally and emotionally abusive to her, although he's never physically abusive. She puts up with it for years, trying to convert him by her sweet spirit and good life. Finally, she consults her preacher about this. He says, "Well, the only solution to this is to pray and pray and work and work towards bringing him into the kingdom of God, because then everything will change."

So they began to pray passionately and deeply and continuously about this. Then, lo and behold, the husband dies. The preacher goes to the woman and says, "I don't know what to say about this." She says, "Well I do. Sometimes God gives us more than we even dare to ask for."

Prayer as Surrender

Sometimes God will give us more than we dare to ask for if we are willing to totally surrender. When we quit trying to manipulate God to get him to do what we want, what we get is more than we could have ever asked for in the first place. What we get is this continuing, abiding presence with God that nothing else he could give us would match.

A Catholic nun told me this story. We often think of monasticism as an individual thing, but it's very much a communal experience. You're living in close quarters with people that you may not share much in common with other than the faith. Anyway, she was telling me about a little boy who went to his mother and said, "I want a new bicycle." The mother said, "We don't have money for a bicycle. Pray for it." But the kid had never prayed before. He didn't know exactly how to go about it. So he started out trying to bribe God. He says, "God if you'll give me this new bicycle I'll be kind and sweet to my little sister." And then he got to thinking about his little sister and he thought, "I'll never get that bike." And so he said, "God, never mind that. If you'll get me that bike, I will clean up my room and keep it clean all the time." But then he looked around that room and he thought, "Getting this bike is going to be harder than I thought." But then another idea occurs to him. He looks over at his dresser and sees a statue of the holy Virgin Mary. He walks over, takes the statue, very carefully wraps it in tissue paper, puts it in a box, puts the lid on the box, ties the box up with string, puts it under his bed, and then commences to pray. He says, "God, if you ever want to see your mother again you better get me that bike."

Now we're not quite that crass about it, but often prayer becomes a kind of cosmic manipulation. "God, if you do this then I'll never do that again," or "You know God, if you're the kind of God you ought to be, you'll do this." But prayer is about something else entirely. Prayer is about entering into the divine life. Prayer is about thinking God's thoughts after him. It's loving what God loves and hating what God hates. It calls for a total surrender.

Prayer and Fatigue

We see this in the life of Jesus, beginning with the very simple prayer that he teaches his disciples to pray. The prayer essentially is from beginning to end a prayer of dependence. Every line expresses human insufficiency and the willingness to surrender oneself to God.

Even the simple physical request is of that kind. "Give us this day our daily bread." If you're a Jew and you hear that, you can only think one thing. Manna. It's a manna prayer. Manna as you recall has a shelf life of twenty-four hours. You get enough manna for that day and only that day. You count on God to do his thing each day, and if God sleeps in the next day, guess what? You go hungry. You live from day to day in dependence on God. God, give me what I need to live this day and I'll count on you to do it again tomorrow. The prayer to be delivered from the evil one recognizes that we have insufficient spiritual resources to take care of ourselves. We need a defender. We need a protector. Every line is dependence.

When Jesus quits teaching about prayer and starts praying, we see it even more. Look at the prayer in Gethsemane. Before I make my main point, I want to make a side point about the sleeping disciples. We make fun of the disciples when they have the opportunity to witness the life and struggles of the Messiah with his Father and they sleep through it. They also slept through part of the transfiguration. Now there's a trick for you.

I comfort myself with these thoughts as I look around my classroom from time to time. I don't mind them sleeping. It's the snoring that really bothers me. I had one preaching student who was narcoleptic. He would sometimes fall asleep in his own sermons. That was hard to recover from.

I think that, aside from our basic disbelief in God, which is fundamental, what hinders us most in the life of prayer is fatigue. I don't think we're so much against prayer as we are too tired to do it. The way most of us live, it is pretty hard for our quiet time to turn into anything else than a nap. Frankly, most of us need the rest. And if we're really going to have a fully developed life of prayer and walking in God, it's not a matter of carving out part of our time to pray. It's a matter of remaking the rest of our lives so we're not so tired that we can't spend some time focusing on God.

For many of us that's going to be pretty hard to do because we've been brought up on the Puritan work ethic and you need to work like mad. One of the things I really appreciated about the hermits at Lebh Shomia is that they adopted what they call God's rhythm. That meant the day began at sunup and it closed at sundown. But with our marvelous technology we can forestall night forever, and so we've lost God's rhythm in our lives. To recover the life of prayer we must relearn that rhythm.

A hermit told me one joke, but I don't think it's funny. He told it to teach me something, and I kind of resented it. He told me about this guy who once a month would go to a person for spiritual direction. One month he felt that he was just too busy. Now how do you call your spiritual director and say, "I'm really too busy to focus on my spiritual life with God at the moment?" He thought about calling in sick and then he thought there's probably something wrong with that. So he finally decided to go but to make short work of it. He decided that no matter what she said, he would say, "I'm fine."

So he goes and she says, "How are things going?" And he says, "Fine. Everything is great. No problems." She says, "Really, everything is going fine?" He says, "Yeah, everything is fine." She says,

"You know, I don't think you've ever come to me when everything was fine." And he said, "Everything's fine. Really there's just no spiritual struggle in my life right now." She just keeps treading the same old ground, so finally he says, "Okay, to tell you the truth, I just don't have time for this tonight. I'm extremely busy and I've got two or three meetings." She says, "Oh, I see. You don't have time. Since you don't have time, perhaps you should just go on and we'll do this another time." He says, "Thanks, okay."

One of the things she had always done is give him Bible verses to think about during the month. So he says, "Okay, before I go give me my verses." And she says, "No, I don't think I will, because you're extremely busy. I don't think you'll have time." He says, "I'm not too busy to think about a few verses. Give me some verses." She says, "Yeah, but if I give you these verses and you're too busy to think about them, you'll feel guilty and that will be even worse. I don't think I'll give you verses." And he says, "Give me the verses." She gives him one. He says, "One verse for the whole month?" And she says, "Well, you're extremely busy."

So in frustration he finally leaves. As he's going out to the car he doesn't recognize the verse she's given him and his curiosity is killing him. So when he gets to the car he flips on the dome light and, as always happens in those cases, it doesn't work. So he turns on the headlights, gets his Bible, gets out of the car, holds his Bible under the headlight to read his verse, and the one verse she's given him for the month is the following: "Are you the Messiah or should we seek for another?"

Now if a hermit told you that story, how would you take it? I took that a little personally. You get the point? You know, when you go to sleep, it's not like the work stops. It's that God comes on duty. It's actually in better hands when you are asleep than when you are awake. If you look at the life of Jesus, who seems to accomplish a great deal, he never gets frantic. He's not running around. He's got some balance in his life and these poor disciples, they're just pooped.

Not My Will, But Yours

That was an aside. That was not the point. Here's the point: "My Father, if it is possible, let this pass from me. Yet not what I want but what you want." Now, it's not enough just to read that. We've got to dwell in the center of that text for a while and then think about how that gets worked out in our own lives of prayer and commitment. My own intuition is that phrase has become for us a hedge against unanswered prayer. What we're saying to God is, "This is what I really want." But then we throw in, "But not my will, but yours," because if we do not get what we ask, we need to have some justification for it. And so we pray for things that we're pretty sure are not going to happen. I don't know about you, but I'm hitting a high percentage of unanswered prayer. When I pray for sick people, they die. We had one young lady in our Nashville church who was in a car wreck. I went to see her and she was a little bit out of it. But she was convinced that since I had come to see her she must be dying. I had to convince her she wasn't going to die.

What we say to ourselves is, "Well, it was God's will for that person to die rather than live." And so we hedge ourselves in this way all the time. We say, "Not my will but yours be done," and then whatever happens, we attribute it to the will of God.

That is not what Jesus is doing here. It's not a hedge. What Jesus is doing is an astounding act for the Son of God. He is totally surrendering. He's going to place himself so deeply in the will of God that, even as God's Son, he's going to say, "My preferences on this are irrelevant. What I want to do is live out the life of God. I'm going to surrender."

Trusting in Resurrection

Now if you're going to surrender to God the key thing is trust. As I read the Gospel accounts, I'm not convinced that the pain of the cross is what's at the forefront here. What is going on here is a much deeper drama in the life of the Trinity than the death of a man on a cross. To be sure, Jesus suffered mightily, but there are human beings who've suffered more than Jesus did. However, if Christian theology is to be believed, there has never been anyone else who bore the sins of the world. As Paul says in 2 Corinthians 5:21, "God made him who had no sin to be sin for us, so that in him we might become the righteousness of God." Admittedly, this is a difficult passage to translate. But if in some sense Jesus becomes the sin bearer, then he does experience estrangement from the Father that he hadn't experienced before, something like the experience of hell. Where do you expect all the sins of the world to go?

In that moment that Jesus becomes the sin bearer and experiences estrangement from the Father, he is counting on God not to abandon him. In all the passages of the New Testament that talk about the raising of Jesus Christ, the resurrection is always the work of God, the Father. Perhaps the Son doesn't have the ability to raise himself. If that's the case, then what Jesus does on the cross is to totally surrender to the Father with the following thought: "I will bear all the sins of the world and then I trust that you will not abandon my soul to Hades but will raise me up." He shows us what it means to truly trust God with everything. Now that's total surrender.

When I look at that, I'm more inclined to admire it than see it as anything I could possibly imitate. So what does total surrender in prayer and in life look like for people like you and me? What does it mean to us? Sometimes you think you know something about prayer and then you go see monks and you know what a kindergartener you are. Talk about prayers. They get up in the morning and they start praying and they pray and they pray and they eat lunch and then they pray and they do a little work and they pray and they pray and then they go to bed and then they get up and then they pray.

I took my spiritual formation group to a monastery one time to go through one cycle of prayer. The monks there do corporate prayer seven times a day beginning at 3:15 AM. And so I was determined that all my guys were going through the full thing. So I was rousting them all out at 3:15 for vigils and one of my guys says, "Do they do this every day?" I said, "Every day, 365 days a year, year after year after year after year." And he said, "Wow!" And I said, "Right." Talk about a life's commitment to walking with God and being changed by prayer.

Surrender as Freedom

As I was talking to one of the hermits at Lebh Shomia, I asked him, "Aren't there times when you don't like to be a hermit? Don't you miss stuff? Isn't there anything you really miss?" At the time I was having an M&M craving. I do not know that M&M's and being a hermit are totally incompatible things but they didn't have any out there. He said, "No, not really." I got to thinking about that. He didn't view the hermetical life primarily through the grid of sacrifice. For him the hermetical life was liberation. It set him free to truly and completely relate to God.

I have frequently used the language of sacrifice. It's highly appropriate. It's in Scripture, but it's not the only way to think about life. I want you to think about things in a little different way for a few moments. Let me give you my own example and I'll try to get you to think about yours. I am by God's calling vocationally celibate. What that means is not just that I am unmarried. What it means is I am unmarriageable. And it has nothing to do with my poor personality. Or total lack of style. That's a different issue.

I occasionally talk to singles groups. Not very often. I don't really like to because it's bothersome to be surrounded by a group of people as pathetic as oneself. I'm kidding. People are single in three ways. Some are single by accident. That's those who are divorced, their spouse has died, or they haven't found that right person yet. Some people are single by choice. They've looked at married life. They've looked at single life and they've decided they like the way single life looks. There are more people making that choice these days.

I was once speaking to a singles group and just on the other side of the wall they had a nursery. As I was speaking we heard a baby crying loudly from across the wall. This went on for maybe five minutes, and so I said, "Let us all just stop and praise God for our choices in life. Because that fine young man is going home with somebody else and we're thrilled about it." Some people just prefer to be unmarried and so they choose single life. They can change their mind anytime they want to. At some point they may decide that marriage is what they want.

Then there's the third category, the category that I'm in, and that is I'm vocationally celibate. That is, I am single by calling and covenant. That is, a long time ago I, for a variety of reasons, sought to devote myself to Jesus and to love him unconditionally without my attention being divided by domesticity. Now if you have this gift, it is a sweet calling. Do you know that I do not answer to anyone besides God and me for my time or my money? It's cool. For most of you that would be an assignment to purgatory. You see, surrendering to God means one thing in my expression of singleness and it means something else in your expression of being married, but in both cases, if we are surrendered to God, we experience it as sweet liberty.

The problem is that married people sometimes want to act like they're single and single people want to act like they're married.

Paul points out that that's a problem. Occasionally I have curious students wanting to know about the single life. I always ask the same question first: "You in a dating slump?" You don't want to make a commitment to the single life while you're in a dating slump. I'm trying to get you to see that total surrender as it's worked out is going to look different for different people, but when we're totally surrendered to God, what we experience is liberating and life affirming because that's the way God is.

And so if one is called to be a hermit, you experience that as walking with God. When you're called to the hustle and bustle of ministry, you experience that as walking with God. In total surrender we find our heart's true home. Now this is going to be pretty hard to do. It's always been hard to do. My guess is it's peculiarly hard to do in American culture where surrender is not in our vocabulary. How is it that we are going to be able to say in the same authentic way that Jesus does, "Not my will but yours be done?" Only from the same vantage point that Jesus does, where you have this deep ultimate trust in God that he will not abandon you and that he raises the dead.

Faith in the Darkness

That brings me to what I really want to talk about. This is tough. I think our problem with prayer is the same problem that we have with the rest of our spiritual life. We have a really hard time believing in God. It's time we put that on the table. We're in the position of that guy in the Gospels who says, "Lord, I believe. Help my unbelief." Preachers are there and elders are there and students are there and Bible teachers are there. My guess is, when we get honest, we're all there.

The biggest obstacle to praying to God is to actually believe that there's any God out there to hear. Sometimes I'm not so sure. I think that's part of total surrender. Part of what it means to surrender to

God is walking in the darkness of faith, not just in its light. I grew up with the notion that faith was following where the evidence led you. What the hermits are trying to teach me is that's not always the way it works. Sometimes to walk in faith is to walk in deep darkness. And their answer to the question, "What do you do when you're having trouble believing in God and you're praying?" is to keep praying.

Lord, I believe. Help my unbelief. I asked one of the hermits what he did when he got tired of being a hermit. His answer was, "I do the next thing." Do you ever have those times when you pray and you don't feel like God's listening or paying any attention or doing anything? I had had a week like that out there in the desert. Do you ever have a week like that? The hermit said, "Week? Just try months. In fact, there was that six-year period back there." I said, "Six years, you're kidding!" He asked, "Are you in this for the long haul or not?" This is not about God responding to every little whim that you have. This is about you walking with God even in darkness.

I think that's the way for those of us who minister. I think it's the only way we can keep our integrity. We go in front of our people and say, "I'm not sure. I've had better days than today with my faith, but I'm going to walk in integrity even when I don't see so well." That's surrender.

You remember *The Prayer of Jabez* book. Now it's not a terrible book. There are some things in that book that could really help you. If you go through life looking for kingdom opportunities, my feeling is that will improve your life. That's one of those things the book suggests that you do. I just have two little problems with the book. Number one, it doesn't have anything to do with the biblical text upon which it's based. I'm a theologian. I'm not too worried about that one. You know, some of our biblical scholars, they're worked up about it. I didn't know Jabez existed until the book. I read those sections of the Bible. I just don't dwell on the names.

The second problem I have with the book is bigger. And that is all the examples in the book are triumphalistic ones. You pray and pow! God gives you what you want. That's not my experience. I had a few of those experiences where I prayed and pow! But usually I pray and it seems that nothing happens.

God didn't talk to Abraham every day. Every time he did he messed up his life. "Abraham, move." "Abraham, sacrifice your son." In the Bible, God never talked to Abraham again after that and my guess is that was fine with Abraham. We have to get over this. Total surrender doesn't mean that you pray and then God hops to and you say, "Praise God." Total surrender means that you walk in your life's calling before God and you do it when you can see well and you do it when you can't. That's surrender.

Surrender that Sustains

You don't think a monk ever has a bad day? A hermit never gets depressed? All of us face dark and troubled times. I want you to have a faith that is going to sustain you through the divorce that you never thought would happen. That will sustain you through the firing by the church you love. That will sustain you through the death of a child. I want you to be so totally surrendered to God that you can say with full conviction, "Not my will but yours be done" and mean it, knowing that God will not abandon you. That what he started he will finish.

When we talk about total surrender we often talk about these super commitments that we make, and I'm not against that. I suppose I'm for it. I'd like us to see a more radical Christianity than we've seen to this point. But what I've learned from the monastic tradition is that there is a far deeper understanding of commitment, and that is, you keep on walking with integrity as God's child even when you don't see much light.

Can you do that? Why don't we quit faking it with each other and not pretend that we don't ever have the doubt or the questions or the fear and then grab each other's hand and say, "I don't understand this. I don't see how this is working out and I don't know what we're doing here, but we will do the next thing. We will walk through this because we believe that if we wind up on the cross God will raise us from the dead." That wouldn't be a bad way to live would it?

I think that if we embraced this perspective, it would change how we pray. My guess is we would be a little less preoccupied with our laundry list and pray a bit more like Paul prayed. What we'll start to pray for is enlightenment and understanding and being filled with the love of God, because that will be far more important than the laundry list of things we want from God. Aside from intercessory prayer that I do, I hardly do verbal prayer at all anymore. I have found that all those things I used to lay on God just don't really seem necessary. I'd rather just be quiet and be there, spending time with the one I love, letting him work in a quiet way and try to walk in slightly greater surrender. And that's a work in progress, because there are plenty of areas of my life that God hasn't taken full control of yet, but we're not done. We're just warming up.

Chapter 3

A MONK WITHOUT A MONASTERY

Many of us want what we see in the monastic experience or the desert experience, but at the same time we are stuck in life and cannot actually join a monastery. So, in the midst of life what do we want to get out of our time alone with God? How do we want it to transform our lives? Once we answer that, I want to talk about how this "monk without a monastery" can become practicable.

A Welcoming Presence

I believe four things should characterize the person who enters deeply into the contemplative life. This is never just about you and God. It's about who you are in the community of faith and among believers. First of all, those who enter deeply into contemplation become deeply hospitable. Hospitality is a dying art. Our initial notion is if people really enter into contemplation, if they've become deeply enmeshed in their life alone with God, then that will make them withdraw from the world. But it's usually just the opposite. They become more hospitable than they were before. They begin to exhibit what I think is the primary characteristic of hospitality in the deepest and fullest sense: a non-threatening presence.

Have you ever been with anybody whose only mode of operation is to try to intimidate? Unfortunately, I run into more than a few religious people of that sort. For them something as simple as conversation is a combat sport. It is a form of fencing. It is a form of intellectual barbarity. The whole thing is about how threatening you can be. In my profession we run into our share of people who want to intimidate you by their education. I suppose those of us who've gotten a bit of it know that there's nothing really to that. There's being educated and there's being smart and they have no relationship to each other. But I suppose you can try to intimidate people by what you know or you can try to help them by being a non-threatening presence.

I had a Christian brother in Nashville whose way of dealing with me was a series of veiled threats. I think our relationship hit its all time low point when he challenged me to a debate over a book I hadn't written yet. And he wrote in his magazine, "I have extended this opportunity to Brother Harris and so far I have heard not a word." The temptation was great to say, "Here's a word: 'Idiot.'" But that would have been ungracious. So I merely thought the thought and did not do the deed. The mere thought made me feel better.

I probably do that sometimes. One of the reasons I try to use a bit of humor in my speaking and writing is because I want to hit you with some stuff pretty hard but I don't want to be threatening to you. I want you to let down your guard. When my students come to my office I don't want to be a threat to them. I want to be a non-threatening presence, someone they can accept counsel from. Someone they know will lay down his life for them if need be.

I've got this peculiar notion that you really learn that in the desert. As you spend time with God you learn how to be with people in a non-threatening way. You learn how to be there for their

well being and for their betterment and for their nurture. I don't
know any contemplatives who play the intimidation game. When
I'm around people who constantly deal with you that way, I can be
pretty sure they don't have much of a prayer life. Think about what
sometimes happens in our churches where we deal with each other
from power. Who's got the most numbers to report? Who's got the
most votes? Who's got the best argument? They're all expressions
of power. And how different it would be if, instead of a point of
view of power, we try to deal with each other from a point of view
of hospitality.

You know the hospitality you like best. It's the people with
whom, when you go into their house, you don't have to have any
pretenses. If you want to, you can take your shoes off. I mean, when
you're in my house, that's the hospitality you will get. I've got dogs.
If you come to my house, you're getting hairy. You don't have to
worry about spilling stuff at my house. I've got dogs. You won't do
anything to the furniture they haven't already done. And that's the
hospitality I like when I go to somebody else's place too.

Learning to Love Sinners

A second thing that characterizes those who enter deeply into the
contemplative life—and you're going to find this hard to believe—is
a missional or evangelistic spirit. My primary problem with being
evangelistic is I don't love sinners. After a little time in the desert
I think I love them more because I begin to stand a little more
toe-to-toe with them. I think I understand at a deeper level that,
but for the grace of God, there I go and there's just not that much
difference in us.

Thomas Merton says that the turning point in his monastic life
was when he took a field trip to Louisville. He was on the streets
with all those people frantically moving around him and he came
to the astounding conclusion that he loved them. Merton had

originally gone to the monastery to run away. He had some tough stuff in his background and it was his way of escape, of closing himself in with God. But when he was in the city he looked around and he realized things had changed. The monastery was no longer his way of escaping from the world, but it had led him to love and embrace the world.

Jesus haunts me in this regard. Talk about a non-threatening presence. I want you to think about this. This is the Son of God and sinners loved to be around him. Now where does that come from? They're not threatened by his presence. They're drawn to it. And apparently his love and concern for them is so palpable that they can feel it. They're drawn to it. And I'm not like that. Here's my old line one more time: Jesus never treats the sinner with anything other than respect. The only people he ever treats with contempt are religious people. So how is it that we treat with respect people Jesus treated with contempt and we treat with contempt people Jesus treated with respect? Perhaps we should pause and ponder that for a few years.

Why is it that sinners don't like me? They don't, generally speaking, because I'm threatening to them. When I lived in Memphis, I would go to an early morning prayer breakfast. One morning on my way, there was a man at my apartment complex whose car had broken down. He said, "There's nobody else out here. Can you give me a ride?" I said, "Sure, I'll give you a ride." And I'm thinking to myself, "I'm going to evangelize him." But somehow I lost the initiative. I hate it when that happens. He was hitting me with a series of questions. I did not want him to know that I was the outreach minister at my church because I thought that would kill my evangelism opportunity. After all, he was a foul-mouthed pagan.

But he said, "What do you do?" I said, "I'm a student." I was in seminary at the time. This is not a line of questioning I really wanted to pursue. He said, "What do you study?" I said, "Philosophy." I did have a philosophy of religion course, so I was at least partially honest. He said, "They pay you to do that?" I said, "No, as a matter of fact, I pay them through the nose to do it." I got caught up in my own pain for a moment. He says, "Well, how do you afford to live in these apartments then?" Not that it took a lot. They were roach-infested apartments. I bought a lizard. That helped. Hey, if you've got roaches, get a lizard. Lizards like roaches. Of course, if you don't like lizards, you might have another problem there. And I said, "I have a part time job." He said, "What do you do?"

Finally I just gave up. I said, "I'm the outreach minister for a church," and it was like this brick wall went up in the car. He had been babbling on. At that point he didn't say another word. He's just been cursing up a storm. I know what he's sitting there thinking. He's thinking of everything he had said over the last fifteen minutes. I was tempted to just curse a little to make him more comfortable.

There's something about Jesus. He didn't have to curse, swear, and sin for sinners to like him. They somehow seemed to know he loved them. So I have a suggestion for myself. And I have a suggestion for elders, ministers, other assorted ministry leaders and dedicated churchgoers. Why don't we cancel all of our elders and staff meetings for the next year, not that anyone would notice. Why don't we cancel all those meetings and make a field trip to the laundromat and the bars and the streets and listen to what makes sinners tick until we love them. I don't mean try to convert anybody; I mean to listen until we love them. Listen until we find ourselves in them. Listen to what they're afraid of, listen to what they hope for, listen to what hurts, until we love them. And then we can try to be the church again.

What do you think? My problem is, I don't know that many sinners, if you don't count students. Let's get out there and find out what makes them tick again. Let's learn to love them the way Merton loved those people he watched out on the streets. Time spent in contemplation with God fuels that, because when you come away from that you say, "Woe is me. I am undone. I am a man of unclean lips and I dwell in the midst of a people of unclean lips." You discover that God loves all of his creatures infinitely and it makes you want to love them too.

I really relate to Jonah. It's my favorite Old Testament book because it's so funny. What a hoot! I mean, Jonah, who doesn't want to preach to anybody, keeps converting everybody. He converts a whole boatload of sailors. Not easy to do in the ancient world. That's just on the way to Nineveh. The problem with Jonah is that the whale gets all of the press. But that fish isn't doing much in the book. The fish is two things. First, it's salvation, not punishment. Read the book. The fish doesn't punish Jonah; the fish rescues Jonah. And second, it's cheap transportation to Nineveh.

I was not taught this story right when I was in Bible school. I just wasn't. I had great Bible class teachers, but they had apparently not read this book closely enough. They taught me that the reason Jonah didn't want to go in the first place was because Nineveh was the capital city of the enemy and he was afraid he would be killed. Which is not true. The book is perfectly clear why Jonah doesn't want to go: he doesn't want to go because (as he says in a snarling tone in the last chapter), "God, I know that you're loving and kind and compassionate and I just knew if I came and preached to this sorry group of people and they repented you wouldn't destroy them and now exactly what I was afraid of has happened." He doesn't want to go preach to them because he wants them destroyed. He hates them. And even after they repent he sits out on a hill hoping that they'll revert back and be destroyed anyway. Never was a preacher so unhappy with his own success.

What a sorry character! God again shows his wonderful sense of humor. He puts Jonah through the ringer in the last chapter and provides him with a shade tree and then he destroys it. Jonah's pouting.

He says, "Oh man, I'm so hot I wish I could just die." And God says, "You seem a little more attached to that green plant than you are to all those people down there who belong to me." The theme of the book is pretty obvious. God loves the Ninevites too. The book doesn't really get interesting until you start asking the question, Who's the Nineveh in your life? Who is it that you hate? Who is it that you don't really want saved? I think we find out a lot about ourselves when get quiet before God and then go out to convert some Ninevites.

Finding Balance

The third thing that happens in time alone with God is that you are able to find spiritual balance above the fray. All of us are deeply conditioned by our circumstances, but we have to be able to find some spiritual equilibrium, some solid ground to stand on. The subtitle of this book is a little unsettling—confessions of a part-time monk. It's not the monk stuff that bothers me. I'm used to that. It's the confessions that make me uneasy, because that suggests that I should let you in and share with you some experiences that aren't my greatest shining moments.

I'm thinking about spirituality above the fray and it got me to thinking how close I came to never having a career in ministry at all. After seminary I went to Syracuse University—for a couple of reasons. I wanted to go to a school where I'd be studying religion with people who didn't believe in it. I knew what it looked like from a believer's point of view. I was interested in what it looked like from somebody who didn't believe in it. One of my seminary teachers used to say, "I want my boys to have a faith so deep that they can go study theology in hell and not lose their faith." I couldn't get into hell, so I went to Syracuse.

But out of the Bible Belt you have a different church situation. So I found myself in this little church, which I then proceeded to help destroy. The leadership was hopelessly divided. They needed somebody of incredible spiritual depth and maturity to help them work through that. Of course, I didn't have any of it. That's a pretty tough situation where the people that you would normally rely on for strength and nurture are part of the problem. I committed what can only be described as ministerial malpractice. It's one of the reasons I have a passion for teaching students because I don't want them to do what I did. Boy, I hurt some people because I wasn't big enough to do the job. Wasn't deep enough to do the job.

And the worst part of it was, I wasn't smart enough to know it. You can't blame a kid for not being mature. You can blame a kid for not knowing he's not mature. It got pretty tough for all of us. We went through some pretty dark days and became isolated from one another. It was just really difficult. And at that point I remembered a little book by a Quaker, Richard Foster, called *Celebration of Discipline*. And it seemed to have something to do with personal spiritual life and finding some grounding outside of all the activities and structures of church. So I went back and I looked at the book and it saved my life. I started practicing those spiritual disciplines that he talks about and I walked through that mess.

I expect my story can be replicated by virtually everybody reading this book. There's been some time in your spiritual life when you've been hanging on by a thread and the usual places of support aren't available. That's where you dig down deep and find God. And you get above the fray and you walk with God through that and you do not go down when things go down all around you. What the church needs most desperately is not better leaders. It's not better preachers. What we need are saints. What we need are people who walk with God so deeply that they are the presence of Christ in our midst. That's what we need. And we need to call our pastors and our leaders and our students to become saints.

So it's not about what church you are a part of. I'm at a lot of churches and they all work at a certain level of dysfunction. Your spiritual wellbeing can't be entirely based on how your community of faith is doing at any particular time. It just can't. There has to be something else. There has to be a depth and a grounding that gives you stability. If I had been a spiritually grounded person when I walked into that situation, things would have been different. I wouldn't have made most of the ghastly mistakes I made.

I'm a great believer in wisdom from God. I just don't think it comes the way we often think it does. I'm not big on God as the supplier of the answers to all the questions I have at any particular time. When you pray deeply and dwell with God, you start to think his thoughts after him and your pastoral judgment gets much better. You quit making so many mistakes because you start to deal with people the way Jesus would. What I really needed at that point was not a course on negotiation or a course on church leadership. What I really needed was to be Jesus. And I wasn't.

I urge church leaders to pay close attention to the spiritual depth of the members of your congregation, especially if you're looking pretty healthy. Because the time always comes when tough stuff happens and conflict arises and what you want to do at that moment is call on the deep wells of spirituality that your people have. And if you go to that well and it's empty, you're dead. We have witnessed this over and over again—when we really needed our people to be Jesus, they were everything but. But you don't turn that on and off like a spigot. You learn that over time by walking with God. That becomes a part of who you are and pretty soon you can't be anything else.

It's also particularly important that we create places in our churches to nurture spirituality, because people are longing for it. I'm not an alarmist in regard to the future of the church, though some who've read my writings think I am. We have people who agree with our doctrine but who are leaving to go find spiritual lives among people whose doctrine they don't believe. Now that irritates me to death. The very idea that you would have to leave a group whose theology you share to go find spiritual life somewhere else. Let our churches be places where we nurture and help people develop their spiritual lives in ways other than just church activities.

Genuine Community

The fourth thing that time alone with God does is to plunge you back into the life of the church. What you discover is that you are not fully complete in your relationship with God until you are at the same time in community with others. Contemplatives need to find themselves involved in the church's life, and I don't think any single individual has to be the church. We don't all have the same gifts, talents, or inclinations, but there is room for all and we need to involve ourselves deeply in the life of the church.

I'm always concerned because many of the people who show the greatest interest in this desert spirituality often have the least patience with the institutional church. Okay, you can see that, right? Because you're in this walking, talking relationship with God and then you go to church and can't figure out what they're doing. And you get this superiority complex. Worship is not spiritual enough for you, the prayers are shallow, and church becomes busy work. You can start to develop a disdain for the community and that's very unhealthy. The challenge is to move back into that church and bring with you the spiritual life to make your contribution to the church. Then you'll receive the contribution of others, because there is no such thing as a solitary Christian.

God's reconciling work was never intended to be about you and God. It was always about us and God. It was always about a new creation. It was about a new people. It's about breaking barriers down, and any spirituality that throws up barriers rather than tearing them down is bound to be wrong.

There was a point in my time at Lebh Shomia that I decided I wanted to be a hermit. I was going to come back and quit my teaching job. I was going to put in my last year as any ethical person would. I was going to quit all the traveling and speaking and I was going to be a hermit. Of course, it's now pretty clear that becoming a hermit was not God's call on my life. And in my opinion, it's not God's call in most people's lives. I don't mind telling you, I have great respect and admiration for those hermits who've spent the last thrity-five years out there walking with God. They're wise people and they share their wisdom. But to most of us the contemplative life needs to be lived right in the middle of the community of faith. It needs to be contemplation that grows, not just out of a deep love for God, but also a deep love for people. This contemplative life becomes part and parcel of our ministry to the body of Christ and to the kingdom of God.

I have concerns about this. I don't suppose anybody sees the foibles of the institutional church more than I do. Maybe you do. If you do, you just have a better foible eye than I do. But I still believe that, in God's plan, it's the only game in town. There can be various expressions of church from megachurch to house church but God calls us into community, into the church. I want to make a suggestion or two about practical ways the contemplative life can become part of who you are.

I'm still working on this myself. I am far from having my hectic life under control. I've built in some regular contemplation times in my life, but I've discovered that's not enough if the rest of your life is a chaotic mess, so I'm working on the chaotic mess side. My desk will be the last part to be brought under the discipline of the kingdom of God. Any of you have my filing system? Look for it until you find it. Do you spend more time looking for it than you do using it when you find it? Oh, yeah.

One of the more annoying facets of my father was his organizational skills. He's one of those people who had those little pencil outlines of his tools in his tool shed and if the tool wasn't on that particular spot he'd have a spasm. And of course every now and again my brother and I would go in there and rearrange them just a little. Sometimes we would just take one tool and move it and then wager how long it would take for him to notice. Soon he'd come in and say, "You all been in my tool shed?" And then we would laugh and he'd know he'd been had again. I once lost the gas cap to his truck and replaced it with another one and I wondered how long it would take him to notice. I hadn't been home five minutes when he said, "You get a new gas cap?" I thought, "What were you doing out there? You haven't even been to a gas station, you know. Did you just go out and check the gas cap to make sure that nobody had changed it?" Oh well, it takes all kinds. Those kinds at universities we call administrators.

Practical Suggestions

Now for my suggestions. Let me suggest first that you start easy and try to build a little contemplation in each day. I'd suggest a half hour is a really long time if you've never done it before, and you might want to work up to an hour at some point. But try to do it at a regular time and try to do it when your biorhythms will let you do it. My biorhythm says that's early in the morning because I'm as good as I'm going to get early. It's the middle of the afternoon where I'm pretty weak. My students seem to work on a completely differ-ent set of biorhythms. I teach 8:00 AM classes and students do not appear to be fully functioning at that point. So if you are not fully functioning then don't do it then. Find a time when you're alert and start to spend some quiet time then.

Second, take advantage of the solitude that your day presents you. If you have a lengthy commute, try doing it without the radio on. Often in our days we have these little spaces of quiet that we feel compelled to try to put some noise in. So let's cultivate some quiet.

When you're home if nobody's watching the TV, you could think about turning it off. Even when people are alone they're never alone. We have all this media going on around us.

Third, if you're really bold, think about taking a one- or two-day personal retreat once or twice a year. Yes, by yourself. Most of us go on retreats, but with most of the retreats I've done lately I'm not sure what about them is retreating. It appears more like a lecture-ship in the woods. The mistake that people who plan such retreats often make is to have someone speak too much. What's the point in having a retreat if all they're going to do is listen to me chatter on? You might want to allow some time for them to actually be quiet and pray and listen to God. So think about getting away for a couple of days. You must leave home to do this. Spend a couple of days and lay your life out before God and reflect on it and see if you're doing what you're supposed to be doing.

There's a saying, "Try not to think, because it slows down the work." We might think about reversing that. We might think about slowing down and seeing which work is worth doing and spend some time in quiet and solitude. Simply take an inventory of our life. And if you're really bold, go a little longer. Take a week. And go do some original research on the existence of God. You do not do this in the library. You do this in the desert. That's where God meets his people.

If you do that, what you have to resist is turning it into a study break. The first thing they did at Lebh Shomia was warn me to stay out of the library. They said, "Look, we know you. You're a college professor. You got forty days here. Your inclination is going to be to spend these forty days reading all the books you haven't had a chance to read, but that's not what you're here to do. That's just another way of hiding from God."

I want to suggest that you and your church find a few people who have these inclinations toward solitude and begin to provide some mutual encouragement and nurture for one another. I find this exceedingly hard to do alone. I think this is so counter-cultural that you need some encouragement and some help along the way.

I guess this is the last confession. What I care about has changed drastically in the last few years. My training is in theology. I spent most of my career trying to apply sound doctrine to the life of the church. I tried very hard to encourage people to build churches on sound theology and not the latest fad. I've tried very hard to get Christians sitting on the pews to be interested in and entertain serious theological discussions because it shouldn't just be happening in the college classroom; it needs to be happening in churches.

And while I haven't lost my passion for that, I have found myself in the last few years agonizing over the problems of the identity and future of the church. I've spoken and I've written on it and I've discovered I have nothing else to say. I'm not sure I ever had anything to say about it in the first place, but whatever I had to say about it I've said. It's public record.

For the few years I have left in my career I'd like to talk about the spiritual life in a way that makes sense to people. A way of thinking about God and prayer and the spiritual disciplines in our lives that will enrich our spiritual lives and our theological discussions. I'm looking for people who want to join me on that quest because it is a great adventure. I'm having more fun in my spiritual search than I've ever had before. A book might not necessarily be the best place to learn about God. You could take a walk with him instead. That might be better. It's a new way of thinking for many people.

CHAPTER 4

FIVE THINGS WE CAN LEARN FROM A MONASTERY

I recently read *Finding Sanctuary*, a book that I highly recommend. It's written by the abbot of a monastery, of course. It argues for getting a saner life by adopting monastic values. I'm going to start out with the assumption that life has gotten a little chaotic. We're a little scattered and most of us are in deep need of some sanctuary in our lives. I want to offer ten monastic values that you don't have to go to a monastery to practice, that will help bring a sanity and sanctuary to our lives.

Why monastic values? Well, this is a way of life that's been sustained for fifteen hundred years. That has something to commend it. And if you've had the experience of hanging out with some of these people, they seem to have a healthy perspective on life. There's a balance there that is admirable. And they didn't just make this stuff up; they actually got it from the Bible.

Silent Listening

Value number one: we've got to build some silence into our lives. We live in an extraordinarily noisy world. To say that my students are overstimulated is putting it mildly. I've told people the most frustrating thing about being a teacher today is there's almost never a single moment when I have a student's undivided attention. They are being constantly bombarded with stimulation and noise and they have a hard time dealing with quiet. As I try to help people in their discipleship with Jesus, one of the first things I try to teach them is to be quiet. That passage in the Psalms, "Be still and know that I am God," at least suggests that it is in stillness and silence that we encounter the living God. I have this notion that God is doing more broadcasting than we are doing receiving. God wants to engage with us. It's just that he's got considerable competition. You've all had that experience of talking to somebody who is not exactly listening. We are so easily distracted that, until we get into silence, we don't even know how noisy our world is.

When I came back from my forty days with the hermits, the first thing I did was to go to Wal-Mart. Boy, was that a mistake! I had never noticed that in people's conversations, they both talked all the time. I found myself walking through Wal-Mart with my hands over my ears going crazy because of all the noise.

Trying to build some silence into our lives is more challenging than you might think. It takes a little planning, especially for those of you who aren't fortunate enough to live by yourselves as I do. You have to make some agreements. I recommend you have at least one chair in the house that when you are sitting in that chair no one is allowed to talk to you. It's the silent place. I also think there needs to be an agreement that one person doesn't get to occupy it all the time! This is not the place where you run when you feel as if somebody's talking to you about something you don't want to hear; it's just a symbol that everybody needs some room to be quiet.

Habakkuk 2:20 is a very important passage to me. Those of you of a certain age have it memorized, even though you don't know it. "The Lord is in his holy temple, let all the earth keep silence before him." That verse has a context. Isn't it interesting when there are contexts? He's talking about idolatry. And he's talking about how in idol worship you say, "Speak to me. I want to hear from you." You keep talking to the idol. When you worship the living God, your first action is not to speak, your first action is to listen, because God is at home and he might actually have something to say. The reason you keep talking when you worship an idol is because the idol is not going to say anything. The only thing that's going to be generated is going to be human. But when you worship the living God, and he's at home, then the first thing you ought to do is shuteth up—because God might have something to say.

I teach preaching. Mine is really the first class where under-graduates preach full sermons and so often I'll get to hear the first full sermon that a student has ever preached. I'll often do that four times in an evening. I don't know if you believe in purgatory, but some of you are going to do some purgatory time when you die. I'm going to skip that. I have already done it.

Every once in a while I'll get that student who has not properly prepared and he or she will say: "I was going to speak on such and such, but the Holy Spirit moved me to speak on this instead." I reply, "Here's a basic rule of mine. The Holy Spirit blesses those who prepare and when God moves he's a lot more likely to move you to silence than he is to speaking." Why do we always assume that the movements of God are toward speech and noise and activity? What God might really need from us is to settle in and shut up and listen. I've been working with a group of young guys who are trying to live out the Sermon on the Mount together. I have this little gong and when I gong the gong everybody immediately goes silent. Because that's the first discipline of worship—learning to be silent.

Reflective Prayer

Value number two goes naturally with silence: the discipline of con-templation or what we might call reflective prayer. This is a form of praying which is not just asking God to bless all the things that we happen to have on our mind, but trying instead to think God's thoughts after him. To try to catch the rhythms of God's life, to pray with Jesus, "Not my will, but yours be done." What if people judged what we thought was important by listening to us pray? They might come to the conclusion that we thought physical health was the single most important thing in the world, because we spend so much time praying for Great Aunt Maude's cancer. But notice what Paul prays about, "I pray that your eyes will be open and that you'll be enlightened and you'll come to understand the love of God in Christ Jesus." He's always praying in the spiritual realm. He's pray-ing that we come more deeply into the heart and the understanding of God. And obviously that goes with silence.

Thus, one of the things that grows out of the silence is this abil-ity to reflect and pay attention to God. There's not enough reflec-tion time in our lives. Many of us come out of activist churches. We're about doing things. But every once in a while we should stop and reflect on whether any of that doing is doing anything. If you will look in Luke 4, 5, and 6, you will find three times where Jesus withdraws for prolonged times of being alone with God. This is a pattern of Jesus' life. He's alone with God and he's out ministering with people. He's alone with God; he's out ministering with people. That's the way Jesus does life. The most interesting of those pas-sages is Luke 5:15-16, where it says people were bringing all sorts of people to Jesus to be healed but he often withdrew to lonely places and prayed. In other words, Jesus walked away from hurting, needy people in order to pray. You've got to give yourself permission to do that, because that's the only way you will ever pray. I don't know if you've noticed, but you never get done with the ministering. There's always one more person who needs you. There's always one more thing to be done, and if you're ever going to pray, you have to walk away from it in order to do it. We just don't get healthy until we accept that rhythm of Jesus into our lives.

So here's the discipline I'm suggesting. Put God on your day planner and then see if anything important enough comes to knock him off. I'm not saying that that won't happen from time to time. In my life it has. There have occasionally come ministering needs so urgent that I broke off from prayer time to attend to them. But that hasn't happened very often in ten years. And if we're intentional about putting God on our schedule and spending time and listening and being with him, then stuff is not going to come along very often that's going to be important enough to knock him off.

I understand that silence and contemplation is going to be easier for some. I know for others this is an extraordinarily difficult thing to do, that you're just not wired that way. I'm not trying to turn activists into contemplatives; I just think we all need a contemplative dimension of our lives. I'm taking Jesus as my role model here.

Liberating Obedience

Number three is the value that I am working on hardest this year: obedience. One of the basic values of a monastery is obedience to the abbot. It's also a clear value in Scripture. Let me admit that I do not obey well. The reason for that is I almost always know best. I won't say I'm perfect, but I'm closer than most. And I think I'm right about everything. So do you, by the way. Think about it. Do you need to pause so you can think about it? We have to get clear about this. Everybody thinks they're right about almost everything. If you don't, you're an idiot. If I ask you why you hold the view that you hold about anything, you will say that the reason you hold it is because you think it's right. If you tell me I hold the view that I hold because it's wrong, I go, "Oh, you're an idiot." Now your past experience has proven to you that you're occasionally wrong, but even those things you were wrong about you have now changed your mind about and you're right again. You also have in the back of your mind that there may be some things that you hold to today that are wrong, but you do not know what those are because, if you did, you would have changed your mind and be perfectly right again. So everybody thinks they are perfectly right all the time.

Now that is an amazingly helpful philosophical concept in your relationships. Most everyone thinks they're right about everything. Which makes obedience extremely difficult, because I sometimes have to be obedient to people who are clearly less informed than myself. Obedience and submission aren't really tested until you have to submit or obey in situations where you're pretty sure you know a better way.

There's this man who has three sons. They're getting ready to move. He sends them off to make preparations for their move and gives them three tasks. They are to build a house, build a barn, and dig a well. And so they go and find the place the father has designated for the house. It's up on a little hill. It's a beautiful view. He's got this great house plan. And so they build the house just like their father told them to. Second, he's got a place picked for the barn down below the house. It doesn't obscure the view. It's far enough so that the smell is not a problem, but it's close enough to be convenient, and so they build the barn just like their father told them to. Then they find the place to dig the well. The father has picked a place a long way from the house; it's very rocky and the water table is really low. They're going to have to dig a long way. And so they find a place that's closer to the house. They don't have to dig as far and it's not as rocky, so they put the well there.

That's not exactly a riveting story. But the question that goes with the story is: "How many times did the boys obey their father?" And our first reaction is two, but of course the correct answer is zero. They did the same thing all three times. They did what they wanted to do. It just so happened that with the first two projects what they wanted to do coincided with what their father wanted them to do. In the same way, we often give ourselves credit for obedience when we do what we've already wanted to do anyway—when the real test of obedience is doing what we don't want to do.

We must obey when God calls us to something that's contrary to our nature—something God does a lot. If you don't think Jesus ever says anything annoying, you are not paying sufficient attention. He calls you to do things that are really difficult to do. I mean, do you always want to take the lowest place, the place of the servant in your life? And so we learn obedience.

Do you remember that strange passage in Hebrews? "Though he was a Son, he learned obedience by the things that he suffered." Which I think suggests that obedience is something that you cannot learn in theory. It can only be learned in practice.

Let me give you one quick example. I always enjoy teaching the story of the rich young ruler in my freshman Bible class. I'm not generally interested in the history of interpretation of passages, but I have spent a good bit of time looking at the history of the interpretation of that passage. And what's interesting is that about 65% of the interpretation of that passage through Christian history is spent trying to explain why the passage does not mean what it appears to. And I ask my students, "Does Jesus really expect this guy to go and sell everything he has, to take a vow of poverty, and to come and follow him?" Half of my students will say, "No, he doesn't mean for him to do that." And I say, "Well, why does he tell him to do it?" And they say, "Well, he just wants to find out if he will be obedient or not." And I say, "How's he going to find that out?" There's only one way you know if you're going to be obedient, and that is to obey. You can't figure that out in theory. That can only be done in practice.

So we learn obedience to God by practicing obedience in other circumstances. That is, apparently the more you obey, the better you get at it. I have to admit, obedience to God is not my best thing either. I am willing to admit that God may know more about things than I do. But that's not always obvious. It's back to this perspective thing again. I don't have a God-like perspective. And it's hard to admit that God may know more about this than I do.

I will occasionally have students who are doing badly in a class that they don't like and one of my tasks in our department is to call that person in and try to get him or her inspired. Of course, this is never in one of my classes where everybody is very enthused. But it will be a youth ministry major taking Greek who can't figure out why this is ever going to matter. I'm a little confused about that myself. I always say to the student, "This is not so much an academic test as it is a spiritual test. This is about learning obedience. And God is going to call you to do all sorts of things in your life that you may not want to do or may not see the point of. And this is a great time to start learning to obey."

You're probably wondering what that has to do with finding sanctuary. Well, as you become obedient, it's amazingly liberating not to have to be in charge of the whole world. You know, to unclench your fist and release things to God and to other people. Obedience is actually astoundingly liberating.

Humble Service

Value number four: humility. Oh, brother! Well, I'm not going to spend a lot of time teaching on humility because it's impossible to teach—and because anything you say about it is going to be wrong. I want you to think about the passage in the Bible that is probably the go-to passage on humility: Jesus' parable of the Pharisee and the publican. He says that two people went to pray. And one says, "Oh, I'm grateful I'm not like that guy." And the other guy just throws himself on the mercy of God and says, "God, be merciful to me a sinner." It's one of those parables that's somewhat like a joke. If you don't get it the first time, there's no point in trying to explain it.

What is humility? Basically, humility amounts to seeing your-self correctly. It has to do with not valuing yourself too much or too little. On the one hand, you are of infinite value because you were created in the image and likeness of God. On the other hand, Jesus teaches that, when you have done your best, at the end of the day you are an unprofitable servant. And if we can hold those two things together, then what comes out is humility. I really love to hang out with humble people. I'm a college professor so I seldom have that opportunity. But what a pleasure and delight it is to hang out with people who aren't hung up on themselves. Of all the values that I see and admire in others, boy, that one's close to the top.

Paul says that Jesus is the example of humility for us. Jesus did not count equality with God as something to be greedily held onto, but instead emptied himself—a literal translation of the Greek—and took on the form of a servant. Emptying one's self is an extremely difficult thing to do. Humility may be like happiness. If you pursue happiness, it's hard to find. Happiness is what hap-pens while you're doing other things. Humility emerges while you're doing other things.

Some fine writers in Christian history have made excellent sug-gestions about how we can start to practice humility. In the little group of guys that I work with, one of our fundamental values is this: "In every situation I will try to take the lowest place." We've even tried to develop eyes to see this. One of the rules we have in our group is that when we get together and food is involved, you are not allowed to serve yourself, nor are you allowed to ask anyone to serve you. So everybody has to watch out for everybody else—ask them what they need and bring it to them. Otherwise, they don't get fed. We're not going to use that rule forever. Our goal is to learn how to walk into a room and immediately look around to see who needs to be served. We want to start meeting people's needs before they even ask.

Can you train yourself to do that? Can you train yourself to be the one who always takes the humble place, the place of the servant? As Jesus washes the apostles' feet, he says, "What I've done for you, you should do for one another." The acts of lowly service help put us in our place.

One of the things I've always struggled with in the monastic tradition, especially the Rule of St. Benedict, is that all monastic rules are disparaging of humor. It was thought unseemly to have a sense of humor. And I get their point. I really do. But it does seem to me that humor is one of the things that can serve humility well. I would like to encourage you to get into the habit of laughing at yourself. Other people are going to anyway; you might as well join in. I try to tell my students, "When you do something stupid, and you will, always tell it on yourself." You would rather spin it than have others spin it anyway. And it is really hard to be humiliated if you have the ability to laugh at yourself. We tend to take ourselves more seriously than we should. I take the cause for which Christ died very seriously. I find it impossible to take myself very seriously.

Covenantal Community

Number five: the value of community. Learning to live with one another in peace or shalom is one of the ways that we find sanctuary. Everybody needs community. And our churches have sometimes served very well in that capacity. Sometimes they have served very poorly. I would like to argue that unless your church is extremely small, you need to find community in a group that is more intimate than what most congregations are.

I have great admiration for the Church of the Savior in Washington, DC. One of their fundamental principles is to stay small. Even if you get big, stay small. Back in the 1970s this church got huge. It got up to about 150 people. And so they immediately broke it up, so that now there are over a dozen manifestations of the Church of the Savior, each with an average membership of a dozen people. They want to be able, in their language, to take "unlimited liability" for the people in their group. How many people in your life do you want to take unlimited liability for?

I usually don't give tests in person to my classes because I don't like to face the hostility. So I'll send a graduate student and I'll go traveling. But one particular day I gave the test myself. I didn't have anything else to do. My co-teacher and I are sitting at the front desk and students are coming up and laying down their tests. A guy comes down and lays down his test and walks out. I look at my co-teacher and I say, "Who was that?" And he says, "Well, that's so and so." And I said, "Is he in our class?" And he says, "Yeah. He doesn't come very much." And I said, "He doesn't come very much? I don't think I've ever seen him before. I thought he just walked in off the street to see if he could do it." He says, "Yeah, he has hardly been here at all." And I said, "Well, why are we letting him get away with that?" I think we were teaching an ethics class. And he says, "You're right. I'll call him."

This is the Abilene Christian University difference. We pursue our students. I have this great game I play in my freshman class. I'll ask if anyone has a friend who's not there they want to call and I'll borrow their cell phone. We'll call the person who's not there and they'll think it's their friend but it will be me and they'll pick up in front of the whole class and I'll say, "Hey, we're waiting for you. Are you on your way?"

So my co-teacher calls this guy and the story that he gives is, "I wasn't there the day you made the seating charts and I don't have a place to sit so I have to sit in different places and that's why you haven't noticed me there." And I said, "Oh, that's ridiculous. I know everybody else in the class. He hasn't been there."

He says, "Do you want to call him?" I said, "Yes, as a matter of fact I do." And so I call him and I say, "What is this story that you're giving? It's bad enough you don't come to class, but then to lie about it. How many times have you been to class?" And he says, "Well, not very many." And I said, "Approximate." And he said, "Two?" I said, "I want to see you. And we'll work out some way for you to deal with the class better. I have a question for you."

I've got the chance for a transformative moment here and so I research him before he comes to my office. I want to know who I'm talking to. He's a little older than your typical student—around twenty-five. And so when he comes in I said, "I want as best I can to lay down my power in this conversation and for us just to talk. You haven't been coming to class. We'll get that worked out. So let's don't worry about that for a moment. This is what I want to know. Are you the person who when you get in trouble will lie about it to get out of it until that no longer works? Is that who you are?"

He paused for a good long while and said, "Well, lately, yes." I said, "Is that who you want to be?" He said, "I don't think so." I said, "Tell me a little about your life."

The story that he told me has haunted me ever since. He was a bit of a wild guy, came from California, of course. He came to ACU, I don't know why. There was some pressure from some direction. And as often happens at our place, he met a girl. He liked her a lot and she was a Christian, and he knew if he was going to have any chance with her, he was going to have to get his life together. You may not think that's the best reason to try to get your life together, but it works for me. And so he started to work on his life. He heard about baptism and that baptism makes you a new creature. He thought, "I could use some of that." So he decided to get himself baptized so he could become a new person. But what haunted him was that it didn't take.

And of course the reason it didn't take is that baptism is not just a personal experience, it's a communal one. We share it in community and he didn't have the people around him to help him live into his new creaturehood. And that's what community does. It's the place where we encourage, nurture, and teach one another what it means to be the new creature. It's the place where we get the support we need to do that.

I think it is extremely difficult to live the Christian life in community. I think it is virtually impossible to do it any other way. And I want to think about how to pull people into deep community. One of the things I've learned since I've been working with these young guys who are trying to live out the Sermon the Mount together is the power of covenant. You're probably aware that covenant is a very powerful word in the Old Testament, the single most important word. In the Hebrew, when you make a covenant you "cut" a covenant, and it probably goes back to the ancient practice that when you made a covenant with a person you would hack up an animal, and the two people making the covenant would walk between the pieces of the hacked-up animal. The symbolism was, if I break this covenant, then what has happened to this animal should happen to me. That's a fairly serious ritual.

I'm trying to bring that one back, by the way. In every wedding ceremony I perform I suggest this one. Hack up an animal, and the bride and groom will walk between the pieces of this hacked-up animal. I thought that this powerful symbolism would make for better marriages—and it would keep the cat population down. You may be shocked to know that I just haven't had any takers on that yet. They don't seem to see the power in it. With the group of guys,there was something about having them sign a piece of paper that said, "I am committed to living life this way with this group of guys," that was extraordinarily powerful, and they've taken those vows very seriously.

The problem is that our church communities are so loose that we never do quite make covenant with one another. We don't say to one another, "We are absolutely committed to living life in a certain way and I'm counting on you to help me do that." I think I have some idea about how hard this is. I spend my life with eighteen- to twenty-two-year olds who are absolutely desperate for community but are largely unwilling to do what you have to do to have it. It takes extraordinary commitment and sacrifice to really have community. We're mostly just flitting in and out and back and forth and have a foot in a dozen different places and never have that group of people with whom we form this deep covenant.

I've been traveling almost every weekend for the last ten years, and that's not a great contributor to deep community. In fact, I am referred to at my home church as St. Elsewhere. I apparently am the only member of that church who attends more often on Wednesday nights than I do on Sunday mornings. But I'm in a covenant group—a group of people who know pretty much everything about me and who, I have no doubt, would lay down their lives for me. And that's where I find sanctuary. They will speak a word of rebuke into my life when I need it, but they love me in a way that they will never let me go. Who is it that doesn't want that kind of community?

Silence, contemplative prayer, obedience, humility, and community. Those are the first five building blocks we have in forming sanctuary. In the next chapter I will give you the last five.

CHAPTER FIVE

FIVE MORE THINGS WE CAN LEARN FROM A MONASTERY

Albert Camus, the French existentialist philosopher, suggested that you spend as much of your life as you can sitting in uncomfortable chairs and standing in line. Because, he says, when you're sitting in a really uncomfortable chair or standing in line life just crawls. You know, time just seems like it's never going to pass. So if you want to make your life seem much longer than it is, then that is what you do.

Which reminds me of this wonderful philosophical joke. A woman is dying. She goes to the doctor and he says, "There is nothing I can do." And she says, "Nothing?" And he says, "I'm sorry, there's just nothing I can do." And she says, "Surely there's something." And he says, "Well, you could marry Randy Harris." And she says, "Will that do any good?" And he says, "No, but it will make the months you have left seem like an eternity." That's our perspective joke for the day. It's all in how you look at things.

And that's what we are doing. Looking at life in a new perspective, through the eyes of the monastic life. Let's look at five more characteristics of monastic life that can somehow be applied to our lives and give us sanctuary in a world that's crazy.

Fearless Hope

Characteristic number six is hope. Our lives work in a much better way if infused with hope. But hope ought not to be confused with optimism. There's no reason to be optimistic. If you are an optimistic person you need to get a grip. Optimistic people are those who do not understand things correctly. I'm of the Benjamin Franklin school. I prefer to be a pessimist and then be pleasantly surprised. The rule of life I try to teach people is "low expectations, few disappointments." So if you come in here with low enough expectations, anything I do will seem fairly good. If your expectations are too high, you're bound to be disappointed.

But the difference is this. Optimism depends on human beings and hope depends on God. And while I don't see any reason to be optimistic, I see every reason to be hopeful. We live in the conviction that what God has started, he will finish. When all the powers of sin and darkness and despair and death have done their worst, God will have the last word. And that makes a great deal of difference in how you live life. I try to convince my freshman students that the complex book of Revelation can be summed up in three simple statements. God's team wins. Pick a team. Don't be stupid. That's what the whole book is about. Yet Christians often don't seem to reflect that fundamental conviction.

I had a young man in my office recently who had lost his faith. That happens from time to time, and we hate it when it happens. They come to a Christian university and lose their faith while they're there. We don't put that on any of our recruiting brochures, but honesty requires me to say, it happens from time to time. This young man has looked around at the chaotic world and just doesn't see how it's ever going to get any better. He's given up. That's where you wish you had that hope pill. You know, give him an injection and renew the notion that God still desires and is working towards the coming of the kingdom in our day and in our world, and there will be a time when God will finish what he started.

Hope allows us to do a great many things. It seems to me that one of the fundamental differences in the contemporary church and the oldest church is we have lost the eschatological viewpoint. We have lost the view that God's breaking into the world is sure and soon. And when you lose that view, then despair is not the only thing that happens. Apathy happens. Cowardice happens. Cowardice is such an ugly word, but one of the things I notice in all the churches I go to is that Christian leaders have become deeply afraid. They're making decisions out of fear instead of hope. It's as if they've forgotten whose side God is on. Hope creates fearlessness in us, giving us leverage on the most difficult times in our lives when the powers of darkness seem to have won. We know that God will not allow that outrage to stand. That puts us in a completely different place in the world.

Many of you have seen books describing what young outsiders think about Christians. It is unfortunate that one of the words that doesn't quickly come to their minds is the word "hope." Whatever else you think about Christians, they should be the most hopeful people in the world. I have to admit that I do not have a hope pill. It's really interesting when you think about it. How do you give hope away? How do you give somebody hope who has lost it? I would like to encourage you to read your Bible with fresh eyes and see how the notion of hope is woven in from beginning to end. It's one of the most fundamental truths taught in Scripture. As I have gotten older I have come to the conclusion that you can put everything important that the Bible teaches on a note card. It's not like the Bible says a great many things. The Bible says the same things over and over and over again. And one of those things that it says is "Hope."

Liberating Simplicity

Value number seven: poverty. If you're not into poverty, let's call it simplicity. One of the basic monastic values is they don't have a lot of stuff. Some of you may be like me recently. You're more familiar with poverty than you were before. My money manager called me right after the crash and says, "I guess you saw what happened to all your investments." And I said, "Well, yes. As a matter of fact I did." And she said, "I just wanted to make sure you weren't getting ready to jump off a bridge." I said, "We don't know each other well enough. You know, suicide has never crossed my mind. Homicide has been a constant thought. And so I would like to suggest that you stay on your side of town until you have different news to deliver."

We all need to simplify our lives. There aren't many good monk jokes, because they are generally opposed to humor. And so this is one of the few. This monk was part of a very strict order where one was only allowed to say two words every decade. That's strict. Most monastic communities do not have a vow of silence. What they do is make a commitment to speak only what love requires—which, by the way, I would suggest for every living human being. Think about how your life would change if you spoke only what love required, and if love didn't require it, you wouldn't say it. That sound like a good idea to you? Be a much quieter world. The guys I'm working with made that commitment for a week and when they came back, I said, "Tell me what you learned." And one guy raised his hand and said, "I'm a very bad person." And I said, "I can see that."

One of the primary ways we relate to each other is through sarcasm and making fun of one another—which among nineteen-year-old guys is a display of great affection. That's the way they say, "I love you." But they got to thinking seriously about what happens when that's the only way you communicate with each other. When everything you say is cynical or cutting or satirical or sarcastic, then you are not speaking what love requires.

Back to the joke. The monk could only say two words every ten years. After the first ten years, he comes to the abbot and says, "Food bad." He comes back after the next ten years and says, "Bed hard." He comes back in another ten years and says, "I quit." And the abbot says, "Well, I'm not surprised, you've done nothing but complain ever since you got here."

We live in a world where bad food and hard beds don't play very well with us. We are undoubtedly the richest, most pampered, whiniest people in the history of the world. And I wonder if there's another way. Richard Foster's best book is the one that is least read. It has the wonderful title, *Freedom of Simplicity.* It is a convicting argument for Christians to simplify their material lives. And he's got the right title. It's not the burden of simplicity, it's the freedom of simplicity.

I do want to make this clear. There is a huge difference in voluntary poverty or simplicity and that which is forced upon you. There is a chasm of difference. Christians have an obligation to practice justice in the world so that those who don't have enough to eat will have something to eat.

But most of us desperately need to simplify our life styles. If you read the Gospels carefully you will see that Jesus talks much more about money than he does about anything else. He talks about money more than he does sex. He talks about money more than he does leadership. I've really been convicted about the Christian obsession with leadership. Jesus talks about leadership almost not at all and when he does, he talks about it almost always in a negative way. He talks about following or submission a lot and almost always in a positive way. The gospel has no interest in leadership. It has great interest in being a follower. Those of you who find yourself in positions of leadership might think about saying to your people, "Don't come follow me, come follow with me. Come follow as I follow."

Just think about all of those topics that we're so obsessed with. Jesus says more about money than he does integrity and honesty. Jesus talks more about money than he does about heaven. And if our concerns reflected Jesus' concerns, we'd be talking a whole lot more about money. "No person can serve two masters. Either love the one and hate the other. You cannot serve God and money." Boy, I really like the old translation on that one: "You cannot serve God and mammon." I didn't know what mammon was, so I thought I wasn't guilty of serving it. Now that new translations have cleared that up, I'm guilty of that one too.

I don't have the formula for simplicity. I've given up trying to tell people what a proper Christian lifestyle is in early twenty-first-century America because I clearly do not know. I am struggling intensely with that in my own life. I work with a group of young guys who've moved into the worst neighborhood in Abilene and they have set up a neo-monastic community there. They call themselves "alelone." That's a Greek reflexive pronoun that means "one another." I simply call them the wild boys. They don't allow personal pronouns in their house. They don't say my car or your car. It's the red car and the white car because they hold all things in common. They wear each other's clothes, which is disgusting because they're not really that much the same size. They've opened up a joint bank account. They have a totally hospitable house. They pray over all their financial decisions. They don't have a television. They don't have internet. They've chosen to live very simply so that everything that they have will be available to other people.

I'm not impressed with all of that. What I'm impressed with is this. If I did that, I think I would be miserable. And they do it and I have never seen them look more happy or free. The freedom of simplicity. Somehow they have it on the inside and now it manifests itself on the outside. And when you just try to work on the outside, but you're not really committed to it on the inside, you might be able to do it, but you wind up resentful that everybody is not making the same sort of sacrifices you are.

So somehow we have to understand that all of these things are passing away. To understand what Jesus says, "God knows you need that stuff, but seek first the kingdom and all these things will be added unto you." I have one suggestion for simplifying our lives. Two words: do something. That's all I want to suggest. You choose, but just do some little something to simplify your life. I'm absolutely convinced that I could get rid of twenty percent of my stuff with absolutely no sacrifice. I wouldn't even notice most of it is gone except I'm not stepping over it anymore. How do you get rid of that much stuff without even starting to make a sacrifice? That would improve my life. So let's do something, even if it's a small something.

Committed Stability

Number eight: stability. One of the things that's impressive about the monastic life is how it has been able to sustain itself over time. But one of the things that we experience in the twenty-first century is a lack of stability, that is, things change so rapidly that it's hard for us to feel as if anything is stable in our lives. One of the better ways to experience stability is to make commitments over the long haul. It seems to me that we have cultivated an ADD culture. We don't have the ability to focus or concentrate on anything for any great length of time.

Follow Me to Freedom by Shane Claiborne and John Perkins is a glorious mess of a book. John Perkins is one of the heroes of the 1960s Civil Rights movement, a cause for which he almost died, and Claiborne is a neo-monastic from Philadelphia. So the young Claiborne is bemoaning the fact that things are not moving as quickly as they need to in his Philadelphia neighborhood. And Perkins response is, "Well, give it ten years." To do anything meaningful requires a commitment of at least ten years. But we've sort of gotten to the point where we'll commit to something for six months and if we don't see the results we want, then we'll flip to something else. And we're just flipping all the time and as a result we don't have any stability in our lives. We don't have any long-term commitments in our lives. Long term to me means ten years. That's about the length of my attention span.

We would get healthier if we committed to fewer things over longer periods of time. Churches ought to be steel when it comes to their mission and plastic when it comes to their methods and structures. But for the most part, churches are plastic when it comes to their mission and steel when it comes to their structures. That is, once a structure is in place in a church, it's almost impossible to uproot it. You get the idea. I don't want to dwell on that one. Because the next one is similar.

Healthy Balance

Value number nine is balance. One contribution to stability is having balance or rhythm in our lives. A couple of summers ago I spent some time at a Trappist monastery. I really like the Trappists. If you want to know what a Trappist is, let's see, how can I explain it? Your basic monk is a Benedictine, but the Benedictines got too lax and so a reform movement started and that was the Cistercians. They were reforming the Benedictines. But the Cistercians got too lax so there was a reform movement that was called the Trappists. So the Trappists are a reform movement on the Cistercians who were a reform movement on the Benedictines. Or to say it another way, Trappists are like monks on steroids.

This particular Trappist monastery has a monastic's associate program. I think it's to see if people are really interested in becoming monks. I explained to them I was not interested in becoming a monk but I would love to be an associate. Being an associate is great. I'm a part-time monk. They let you come in. You keep the exact same schedule that they do. So you go to your cell when they go to their cell. And you work with them and you pray with them. You get up at 3:30 in the morning to pray vigil. The day starts very early in a monastery, but it's easier because there's no night life. You go to bed rather early because there's just not a lot to do. I got to stand with the monks and chant the Psalms, which was just an absolutely amazing experience.

So you go to meals when they do and then you go to your cell to read and study, not to get back in the bed. Once you get up you are not to go back to bed. They emphasized that to me. And so you'd read and study for a while and then you'd come back and you'd pray together again. Basically the mornings were dedicated to prayer and reading and in the afternoons you'd go out to work with them. And it was farm work. I am not a farm boy. So they had to give me fairly specific instructions and even then things didn't always go that well. I learned how to shuck corn. Dig potatoes. Pick tomatoes. When they sent me out to cut down a tree, that's the part that didn't go well. I cut down the wrong tree. And if you're not aware of this, monks can get angry. It's not like they don't have any temper at all.

We'd be working and the bell would ring calling us to prayer and guess what we would do? Drop everything and go pray. Then at night we would chant compline and we would go to bed. And it's just this remarkable balanced life where there's time for prayer and there's time for sleep and rest and there's time for work and there's time for meals and none of it ever felt rushed. There was room for everything.

I wonder if we could learn to do that? If we could find this balance and rhythm in our lives where life never feels rushed? My favorite spiritual book of the twentieth century is Thomas Kelly's

A Testament of Devotion. Kelly emphasizes the point that if you find yourself in frantic, feverish activity, God didn't call you there. Because he never does. He calls you to peace. And if you're living that life, you got there some other way. You didn't get there by the call of God.

I am desperately looking for some balance in my life. But it hasn't been going very well. I pray a lot. I think I'm probably ahead of most of you in the prayer sweepstakes. If prayer will get you into heaven, I'm good. I'm hoping there are two things on the test. Prayer and going to church. Because, boy, have I spent some time in church!

But the problem is, I create all these spaces for prayer in my life and it happens, but then the rest of my life is absolutely chaos. Any of you have that experience? I go into my wreck of an office and there's just chaos everywhere. I don't have the gift of administration. I have that filing system where you look for it until you find it. I spend more time looking for stuff than I do using it. And my travel schedule has been absurd and I feel this deep longing for balance.

I think that's God's call to us. We're trying to make an appeal to the world for the kingdom of God and I think the world would often say to us, "Why would I want to trade in my sort of craziness for yours? I don't see much difference. You're as driven and as unbalanced and as crazy as I am. It's just I go to the club and you go to church." So maybe it's time for us to try to find that balance in our lives, to believe that there is plenty of time to do everything God has called us to do. One of the ways I tried to start building this into my life is through the great spiritual discipline of walking. You may have noticed that a whole lot of really important stuff happens in the Bible when people are walking. And absolutely nothing important happens in the Bible when people are driving.

One of the things about driving is everyone else who is driving is a natural enemy. And it's not a very communicative means of transportation. There are certain things you can communicate, but you shouldn't. There is no universal sign for, "I'm sorry. I know that was stupid. I hope I didn't ruin your day." There are signs that convey other sorts of messages. But when you're walking, generally speaking, anybody else who is walking is a comrade, a person on the way. When I say walking, I'm not really talking about walking—I'm talking about strolling.

I power walk almost every day. I walk four miles a day and this is not a time when I want anyone to speak to me. I have strategies to keep that from happening. I have the iPod earphones; I just don't have the iPod. I put the earphones on; I put the cord in my pocket. People think I'm listening to something and they won't speak to me so I can walk.

I'm not talking about that. I'm talking about strolling. And so I have accepted the discipline in my life that whenever I have a meeting somewhere across campus I will always leave ten minutes early and stroll and see what conversations I can get in between my office and wherever I'm going. This has been a wonderful experience. When I'm walking along, I keep my eyes open. I see a couple of students over there studying their Greek and I'll stop and say, "Hey, how's it going?" and they're always ready to talk to me because they hate Greek. I go outside and students are doing slack line. You know what slack line is? You set up this cord and then tie it between two trees and you walk across it. And they say, "Hey, come and walk on the slack line with us." And I say, "Sure." So I throw off my shoes, and get on the line—which doesn't go that well.

I have these great conversations and I discover that if I have my head up and I'm strolling, there's all this stuff going on around me; I can just take my time and listen and pay attention and I'm so much happier when I get to the meeting. I get there and I know probably none of it's going to matter. What mattered was the stroll over. It was just this realization about how out of balance so much of my life is. I've got my life so scheduled that if somebody really needs something, I say, "I'll put you on my appointment calendar a week from Tuesday." My friend Mark Love talks about having life shaped in a way where you are available for divine interruptions. Most of us need to flex our schedules so that if God brings someone or something into our life that we actually have the time to attend to it.

I'm not particularly good at playing. I'm trying to get better at it. You'd think hanging out with students all the time I would be better at it than I am, but often the ways I've tried to play are very stressful. Golf—have you ever tried that? I mean, trying to get that ball in that little hole? I know why they call it a stroke! There are ways to play that don't create additional stress. Even the way Americans vacation—they do it in such a way that they see how much stress they can create while they're on vacation. The call of God is to peace and stability and balance.

Welcoming Hospitality

Number ten, the last characteristic, is hospitality. I know you don't think about monks as being extremely hospitable. But I have to tell you, they are some of the most hospitable people I have ever met. If you go pound on the door of a monastery at midnight tonight, you know what they're going to say? They're probably going to say, "Yeah, you can come spend the night." Because they're afraid that if they turn you away, you will turn out to be Jesus. And don't you hate it when that happens. That really is the key to hospitality—seeing Jesus in everyone. And how do you want to entertain Jesus?

Hospitality doesn't just have to do with inviting people into your house, although that is a wonderful way to do hospitality. Sometimes hospitality means being willing to go to theirs. I have to tell you, it's a lot easier for me to invite students into my house than it is for me to go over to the dorm. But every once in a while hospitality requires me to go over on their turf and be where they are. One of the harder things is for me to be a hospitable presence in my office. People will come to my office and the first word out of their mouth will be something like, "I know you're really busy." Bad start. So very quickly I have to let them know that of course I'm busy, everybody in the world I know is busy. But while they're in my office there's nothing else I need to do. There's no one else I'd rather be with. There's nothing else I would rather be doing. That's what it means to be hospitable, to be a welcoming presence.

I teach ethics, among other things. The worst ethics class I ever taught was because I had a couple of intercollegiate debaters in there. I had a little bit of that in my own background and unfortunately they sometimes come to view conversation as blood sport that has one goal: to win. And I never could get them to understand the concept that what you are trying to do is to keep the other person talking. The goal is not to shut them down. The goal is to make them want to continue the conversation, because when you quit trying to win and actually listen then the truth has a way of emerging. And I can tell you, there are a hundred ways to shut people down and far fewer ways to keep them talking.

Does your church shut people down or does it keep them talking? To be a hospitable presence means that the other person is welcome in your space and that you want them there. Hospitality was one of the marks of early Christianity. That whoever came was welcome was one of the signs of Christians. The love feast was a fundamental symbol of Christian hospitality. So let's ask, "How do I become a welcoming presence to people? How do I make them comfortable?"

Let me use one daring example. A couple of summers ago I decided I wanted to learn something about Buddhist meditation. Don't make more out of this than it is. I'm not interested in becoming a Buddhist. I love Jesus. But when it comes to sitting, being good sitters, I think the Buddhists are the experts. Best sitters in the world. And if you want to learn to sit, they're the people you learn from. So I go to a Buddhist monastery. I've been to all sorts of Christian retreat centers and monasteries and hermit's places and I'm immediately comfortable there because we share this common theology and commitment to the lordship of Jesus Christ. But I am nervous and I know there are very specific rituals that go with Buddhist meditation. I'm just wondering how this is going to go. And it's hard to explain what it means to have people who are really hospitable to you in those circumstances. Who never make you feel stupid. Who do everything to make you feel included. Who teach without talking down. Who welcome you into their community for the time you're there.

Or I think about when I was at Syracuse University going to school and one of my best friends there was an atheist Marxist anarchist. He's also the most brilliant person I've ever known. I do not know whether he's teaching at some school or is in prison. He would frequently have student gatherings over at his house and he would never touch a carbonated beverage. Never. He would touch fermented beverages. I'd go over to his house, open the refrigerator and there's Coke sitting there and it's for me. I'm the only non-drinker in the group and so he keeps stuff in his refrigerator that he would never touch for this one person. No Christian commitments at all, but a deep understanding of what it means to make people welcome. And then I started asking myself, "Well, would I keep beer in my refrigerator for him? How does this work here?"

I've been thinking about the way Jesus had of welcoming every-body into his presence. Little children and sinners and prostitutes and the poor and Nicodemus would run to Jesus. He seemed to have this way of creating space for everybody, making them feel welcome in his presence, and I can only figure out one way he did that. They *were* welcome in his presence. You can't fake this. You either want people there or they'll know you don't. And if I really want them there, then I can do things to be a welcoming presence. I would give anything if people would say about Christians, "You may love them or hate them, you may agree with them or disagree with them, but of all the people in the world, they are the most welcoming. They always let you know that they're glad you're there."

Maybe that's where the monastic disciplines take hold with mission, the other thing I'm really concerned about. How do we start to reach those parts of our culture that we haven't reached yet? One of the questions you have to ask is, "Do you want those people here? Do you want to be with them? Do you want to have them messing up your stuff? Are we going to be a hospitable presence?"

What lies behind everything I've said is the fundamental conviction that being a follower of Jesus Christ has very little to do with going to church and a great deal to do with the transformation of our lives. And unless we start living qualitatively different lives in the world, the message that we speak has no credibility. I'll just offer an opinion. For the most part, the problem has not been that we have the wrong message; the problem has been it has been attached to the wrong lives.

CHAPTER 6

NINETEEN WAYS TO BE HUMBLE

Pursuing humility is a little bit like pursuing happiness. It's one sure way not to get it. Happiness and humility are things that happen while you're doing something else. I was thinking about the children's Bible class teacher who was teaching through the Gospels and came to that passage about the tax collector and the Pharisee praying in the temple. The Pharisee says, "I'm glad I'm not like other men," and the tax collector says, "Be merciful to me a sinner." The take away line from the teacher was, "Now aren't we glad we're not like that Pharisee?" You get to thinking about that, and it doesn't quite work, does it?

So I did what scholars do when assigned a topic that one clearly knows nothing about. I read people who I thought might know. So I thought I would spend a little time with Jeremy Taylor, then Jesus.

I know that seems backwards, but I want to talk first about some people who give rules for being humble. They believe it is possible to act your way into a better way of thinking. That's not generally the way we think, but we've had some success at that. We've had to go do something we really didn't want to do, and we did our best to throw ourselves into it, and we managed to act our way into a little better attitude. I'm not quite saying, "Fake it until you make it." I'm not talking about hypocrisy. What I'm talking about is commitment and obedience—the willingness to pursue a way of life even when you're not real crazy about the idea in the hopes that it will grow on you.

The reason I chose Jeremy Taylor is because he is brilliant at looking inside of us and catching us. Don't you hate those people? You know, the ones who have this x-ray vision and know what you're really up to. I'm glad he's dead. I'm going to spend most of my time just thinking through Jeremy Taylor's rules. But for those of you who like context, his years are 1613 to 1667. He was English and lived in the time when England was going back and forth between the Catholics and the Protestants . He spent some time in prison but wound up being a bishop.

He's best known for two books. One is called *Holy Living* and the other is called *Holy Dying*—who couldn't be drawn to those titles? In *Holy Living* he gives nineteen rules for living humbly. What a strange number! I'm going to go through these rules, not so much to offer Jeremy Taylor's commentary on them, but to offer my commentary so that you'll see something about what I think, as well as what Taylor thinks.

Number one: "Do not think better of yourself because of any outward circumstance that happens to you." Okay, let's stop there. I have occasionally said to a student, "The problem is you were born on third base and think you've hit a triple." A whole bunch of us were born on third base. You know, I didn't choose where I was born. I didn't choose to whom I was born. I had the good fortune to have parents who weren't wealthy but believed in hard work and who believed in God. I grew up in an environment that was safe and stable and I didn't do any of that. You cannot take credit for your circumstances when you didn't do a whole lot to create them. I don't think there are any self-made people. All sorts of circumstances conspire to make us who we are.

One of the examples Taylor gives is that some horses just run faster than others and you can't take credit for being a horse that was born to run a little faster. Let me give you an example from my own life. I am not the brightest bulb on the Christmas tree, but I've discovered that I can learn things relatively quickly. When I moved to Tennessee, they had a rule that you had to take a written driving test in order to get a Tennessee license, whether you had one from another state or not. I didn't realize that until I got to the license bureau. I said, "Well, what is the test about?" And they said, "Uh well, driving." And I said, "Okay, I might have guessed that." I assumed it wasn't an algebra test. I said, "Is it basic rules of the road, because those tend to be similar in all places, although everybody's got their own local take on them?" They said, "A large percentage of the test is about the drunk driving laws in Tennessee." I was not familiar with those laws because that's never been a problem to me. So I said, "Okay, give me the driver's handbook." I took the book and spent twenty minutes reading it, and said, "Let's go." I took the test and passed it.

Aren't I brilliant? All around me I'm seeing people who are taking this test for the second, third, and fourth times and struggling to pass it. How much credit do I deserve for being able to read a book quickly and pass a test? That's just like a horse being able to run fast. It's not anything that brings you credit or worth, just something you happen to be able to do. I've discovered there may be another area or two in which I'm not quite as gifted. No one has really appreciated my basketball prowess as they should. For instance, one of my great gifts to basketball is I help other players' rebounding statistics. It's all a matter of how you frame it. That a person would deserve any credit or honor because they're athletically gifted is nonsense. That's all external circumstances. Someone else is lucky enough or gifted enough to make money; none of that has anything to do with our character or who we are.

Number two: "Humility does not consist in criticizing yourself for wearing ragged clothes." I'm disappointed in that one. "Or in walking around submissively wherever you go. Humility consists in a realistic opinion of yourself, namely that you are an unworthy person." That comes from a certain era and we wouldn't put it quite that way. But this self-esteem thing has gotten a little out of hand. Every once in a while we need to go back to the Gospels and say, "When we've done everything we can do, we are still unworthy servants." It does seem to me that a realistic opinion of yourself is really helpful.

Number three, and I really like this one: "When you hold this opinion of yourself that you are an unworthy person, be content that others think the same of you." I just have to read a little bit more of the Taylor commentary because it's so good. "If you realize that you are not wise, do not be angry if someone else should agree. If you truly hold this opinion of yourself, you should also desire that others hold this opinion as well. You would be a hypocrite to think lowly of yourself but then expect others to think highly of you." Is that good or what?

Fourth: "Nurture the love to do good things in secret concealed from the eyes of others and therefore not highly esteemed because of them." Some contemporary writers like Dallas Willard say secrecy is one of the spiritual disciplines. My guess is he may have gotten that from Jesus. "When you're giving don't let your right hand and left hand know what's going on between each other." This doing things in secrecy is one of the best ways to check our motives. That is, if I'm only willing to be generous when the lights are blaring and people are going to see, that's one thing. If I'm willing to do things in secrecy that no one is ever going to know then that's one way of checking our motives. Just do secret acts of kindness. It is a lot of fun. People try to figure out who is doing it; they'll give credit to somebody else, and it just spreads good will.

Number five: "Never be ashamed of your birth, of your parents, your occupation or your present employment or the lowly status of any of them." I wish that we could say that we Christians were free of the perils of status, but we don't seem to be. This one speaks for itself, I suppose.

Number six: "Never say anything directly or indirectly that will provoke praise or elicit compliments from others." What would it be like to go through a day and try to have a compliment free day? One of the things that several of these rules have to do with is what we postmoderns would think of as power plays in language. Think for a moment about how we use language and how it works. I am trained by postmodern theologians and philosophers and they are of the opinion that almost everything is power play.

I'm not going to go quite that far, but almost. We manipulate people and conversations to come out in a way that is agreeable to us. Let me give you two or three quick examples and then get back to Jeremy Taylor. I do a lot of speaking. Occasionally people have the bad sense to let people ask me questions after I've spoken. The key to question and answer sessions is, no matter what question the person asks, to answer the question you want to. A person gifted at this will take the question the person asks, massage it until it's the question they want to answer, and then make the person think that's the question they asked. If you watch people in public life who are used to doing question and answer sessions, you will see that happen over and over again. Sometimes I'm among audiences who ask a question that I don't want to answer. It's rude to say, "I don't want to answer that." So I sort of answer, that is, I take control of the conversation.

Politicians are good at this. I'll give you my favorite example. For years we had that missile system in Europe aimed at the Soviet

Union and the Europeans always had mixed feelings about it. On the one hand, they liked the protection. On the other hand, it also made them a target. I don't know if you remember the name of these missiles. These were Pershing missiles, but they were called "Peacekeepers." Talk about a power play. Now if you're going to put a missile system in Europe, Peacekeeper was a good name for it. (Just try getting congressional approval for a missile system called, "Baby Killer.") The plain fact is they're the same missiles whether they're called peacekeepers or baby killers, right? So what we do is use language to try to assert power.

I think part of what Taylor is after here is the way we manipulate conversations to stroke our egos. This is one of the places where I think he really catches us. For instance, when I'm in a conversation with people, I think of how I can move the conversation to an area in which I have greater expertise than they do. Even in those places where I am trying to show humility, what I'm really trying to do is to say, "Well, you know that just really wasn't my best sermon. You know, I just didn't quite have it today." The last thing I want them to do is agree with me. What I'm doing is baiting them to say. "Oh, that was a fine sermon." If they should agree with me that it was not a very good sermon that's apt to ruin my day.

Pay attention to how we use language to congratulate ourselves. Try this experiment. Choose a day when you know you're going to be deeply involved with people, and on that day try to work every conversation in such a way that it is going to build up the other person and not yourself. That is, do a reverse power play. I'm going to keep moving the conversation so the other person will be built up and encouraged and edified. I want to deflect attention away from myself. And I'm going to do it in a way that it is not going to reflect good on me that I'm deflecting the attention. That's the tricky part.

Number seven: "When you do receive praise for something you have done, take it indifferently and return it back to God, the giver of the gift, the blesser of the action, the aid of the project. Always give God thanks for making you an instrument of his glory for the benefit of others." That's really well said. One of the hardest things about teaching preaching students is to encourage them without doing it too much. One of the hardest things as a preacher is to know how to take a compliment. Now I like compliments. I would prefer when I'm finished preaching that somebody would say, "That was good," rather than saying, "It stunk" (or stank or whatever the proper verb form there is). But I remember very early in my own preaching career a great gift was given to me by Harold Hazelip, the dean at my seminary. I'd made a speech. I must have been twenty-four at the time, so you know I had absolutely nothing to say. Afterwards he said, "That was really good." That was the first gift—encouragement from a man I had incredible admiration for. Then he gave me a second gift. He said, "That was really good; now let me give you a piece of advice. Never take your public seriously."

Number eight: "Make a good name for yourself by being a person of virtue and humility." Well, that's what this is all about so I don't find that all that helpful, do you?

Number nine: "Do not take pride in any praise given to you. Rejoice in God who gives gifts others can see in you but let it be mixed with a holy respect so that this good does not turn into evil." Well, that's the same thing as number seven. It's just said in a different way.

Number ten (which is very close to number six): "Do not ask others your faults with the intent or purpose being to have others tell you of your good qualities." Okay, we're back to that power play in language where I'm not going to be fishing for compliments by telling everybody how bad I am.

Number eleven: "When you are slighted by someone or feel undervalued, do not harbor any secret anger, supposing that you actually deserved praise and that they overlooked your value or that they neglected to praise you because of their own envy. Do not try to seek out a group of flatterers who will take your side and whose vain noises and empty praises you may try to keep up your high opinion of yourself." That's a big one because it is really easy for us to feel undervalued, underappreciated, and slighted. Taylor's point is, if you really come to believe that when you've done your best you are an unworthy servant, then it is impossible for you to be undervalued. And so whenever people do that it doesn't have any power on you because you know they're right.

Let me briefly address those who are in my profession. I'm talking about preachers. I cannot tell you how many preachers have told me that the reason I know nothing about humility is because I'm not married. For preachers, the key to humility is a spouse who'll let you know, when you think you've preached a pretty good sermon, that it wasn't all that good.

I do think that ministers are a strange and dangerous combination of pride and deep inferiority complex. I know hundreds of preachers and most of us fall into that category. On the one hand, you stand up in front of several hundred people for an hour, which is 250 hours or over ten days of their time. That is really nervy. On the other hand, those of us who preach have the great misfortune of knowing the preacher better than most. We know the deep flaws and problems in our own lives—and the ones we don't know, others generally will point out to us. So you wind up having this combination of pride on the one hand and inferiority in the other, and it is a volatile combination.

So when we get one of those slights, when we're under appreciated or undervalued, regardless of how people mean it, let's take it as God's gentle discipline. Let's take it as a way of keeping things in perspective. Let that be the reminder that when we've done our best we are unworthy servants; and it doesn't matter how they mean it, that's the way we can take it. I think we will become better people for that.

Number twelve: "Do not entertain any of the devil's whispers of pride such as that of Nebuchadnezzar, 'Is this not great Babylon which I have built for the honor of my name and the might of my majesty and the power of my kingdom?'" Kingdom building is a dangerous business. The only one who builds a kingdom is God. We're just laying a few bricks.

Number thirteen: "Take an active part in the praising of others, entertaining their good with delight. In no way should you give in to the desire to disparage them or lessen their praise or make any objection. You should never think that hearing the good report of another in any way lessens your worth." If we have a moment of deep and sudden honesty, again Taylor catches us here. We all have had a moment when we heard about somebody's failure and everything in you said, "Yes!" Or we've had a moment when we heard about somebody's success and everything in us says, "Too bad."

Number fourteen is similar: "Be content when you see or hear that others are doing well in their jobs and with their income even when you are not. In the same manner be content when someone else's work is approved and yours is rejected." Boy, that's tough.

Number fifteen: "Never compare yourself with others unless it be to advance your impression of them and lower your impression of yourself." I don't like to do that. In fact, I like to compare myself to people in areas where I'm clearly superior. In fact, when it comes to power plays, if I'm talking to people who are clearly superior in one area I will shift the conversation to another area.

I've done this for years. I have one foot in the church and one in the academy. I've got them both planted pretty solidly and have some ability in both. But when I am in a group of scholars, I know I am inferior and so what I do is shift things over to preaching because most scholars don't preach well. That's why they're good scholars. Or if I'm in a group of preachers and they're really good preachers, then I will shift to scholarship because they're usually bad scholars. That's what makes them good preachers. And woe be unto me if I ever get into a situation where I'm with preaching scholars. Then what am I going to do? I'm going to talk about football.

Taylor says that, if you're going to compare yourself to somebody, always do it to lower your impression of yourself, not raise it. Again, speaking out of my own experience, when I went out to the hermits' community several years ago to pray for forty days, one of the things I discovered was the truth of Isaiah 6. When you're not allowed to speak and when there aren't any other people around to compare yourself to, when there's nothing but you and God's holiness, what you discover is this: "Woe is me, I am undone. I am a man of unclean lips and I dwell in the midst of a people of unclean lips for I have seen the Lord." We can keep comparing ourselves to other people in ways that enhance our stature, or we can look at ourselves as opposed to God's perfection and glory and then see ourselves as we really are. You know, maybe Jeremy Taylor's got something here. We have to look around and find those people who make us want to reach higher.

Number sixteen: "Do not constantly try to excuse all of your mistakes. If you have made a mistake or an oversight or an indiscretion, confess it plainly, for virtue scorns a lie for its cover." Or to put that in modern terms, "It's not the crime that kills you, it's the cover up." A couple of years ago, a hockey player had bashed somebody's head into the ice and gotten suspended for the rest of the year. His apology was stunning because he managed to apologize but didn't apologize. This was the language: "I'm sorry for what happened." Interesting. Passive voice. He was absolutely not taking responsibility. That is a completely different thing than saying, "I'm sorry that I assaulted a guy on the ice."

Why is "I was wrong" so hard for us? Of course, what I really hate is when it's a student; you know, that's just almost intolerable when they're right and you're wrong. But sometimes that happens—or at least it might.

Number seventeen: "Give God thanks for every weakness, fault, and imperfection you have. Accept it as a favor of God, an instrument to resist pride and nurse humility. Remember if God has chosen to shrink your swelling pride, he has made it that much easier for you to enter in through the narrow way." Yes, thank God. Thank him for every weakness, fault, and imperfection that you have. Well, you've heard the old joke, "I used to be conceited, but now I'm perfect and I don't have that problem anymore." What would we be like if we didn't have those imperfections in our lives to remind us?

Number eighteen: "Do not expose other's weaknesses in order to make them feel less able than you." We've covered that ground I think.

Number nineteen: "Remember that what is most important to God is that we submit ourselves and all that we have to him. This requires that we be willing to endure whatever his will brings us, to be content in whatever state we are in, and to be ready for every change."

I would be really curious about how you react to a list like this, because we've done a pretty good job in recent years of insisting that lists of rules are, in principle, bad news. That they somehow make us legalists or somehow reflect adversely on God's graciousness. But I tell you, I find Jeremy Taylor's stuff to be really insightful and helpful. I go back and read this every once in a while; it helps me practice my way into a better way of thinking. If I did these sorts of things for a while, then I might have a more sensible view of myself and the rest of the world.

CHAPTER 7

HUMILITY THE JESUS WAY

Since I know little of humility, I've been stealing from people who I thought might know something about it. I thought I might steal from the Bible. I'm going to start out with a passage from Jesus and then I will look at a couple of passages that are reflections on Jesus and the place of humility in his life.

Let's start with something that Jesus said in the Sermon on the Mount, Matthew 5: "When he saw the crowds, he went up on a mountainside and sat down. His disciples came to him and he began to teach them saying . . . ." And these are the first words out of his mouth—"blessed." Does that sound like a command to you? That doesn't sound like a command, does it? He gives some difficult demands before he's done with this sermon, and you're probably familiar with those. But before he ever gives a command, the first thing he does is pronounce words of blessing.

Poor in Spirit

The first group he blesses is the poor in spirit. Okay, who are the poor in spirit? When I was a student in college I played intramural sports like almost everybody did. I signed up for a softball team. They put twelve people on a team because usually somebody couldn't be there, and as you know in slow pitch softball you play ten people. So in one particular game my team is in the field and I look out there and discover that my team is playing with nine players and I'm sitting on the bench. You haven't been properly insulted until you realize your team would rather play shorthanded than have you out there anywhere. It's a little hard not to take that personally.

That's not the only time that's happened in my life. A few years later I applied for a job at my seminary. I did not get the job. That's not the bad part. The bad part is they decided to hire nobody. It's one thing to finish second to a real candidate, but it is hard not to take personally finishing second to nobody. "You know we would rather just not fill this position than fill it with you." Now I've gotten pretty close to describing the poor in spirit.

One of my mentors suggested that you should think of these people as those left behind when Israel was taken into exile. They were the people they left on the bench. They're the people they left in the land, because you haven't been properly insulted until your nation's been hauled into exile and they say, "We won't need you." These are the people to whom Jesus says, "Blessed."

I'm just thinking those people must have heard that as good news. "Blessed are the poor in spirit, for yours is the kingdom of heaven." And that sets me to wondering. What is there about being poor in spirit which is a virtual equivalent to humble? What elicits this blessing from Jesus? Surely it is because these people can make no claims on their own. These are the people who have nothing to offer, and God's word to them is, "You are blessed."

It gets me to thinking about what Jesus said to Nicodemus: "You must be born again" or "You must be born from above" or "You must be born anew." It can be translated any of those ways. We quickly move towards turning this into a baptismal passage and perhaps it is, but it seems to me what he's telling Nicodemus is the only way to enter the kingdom is as a baby. All of those honors and all of that knowledge and all of those things you have going for you as a Jewish leader, you have to leave them behind. Because when you come to Jesus you come empty handed.

Humble Yourself before Others

Let me start with the easier passage and work to some more difficult ones. First, Philippians 2, which is an early Christian hymn that Paul may have massaged a bit. It says,

> In your relationships with one another, have the same
> mindset as Christ Jesus:
> Who, being in very nature God,
> did not consider equality with God something to be used
> to his own advantage;
> rather, he made himself nothing by taking the very nature
>   of a servant,
> being made in human likeness.
> And being found in appearance as a man,
> he humbled himself
> by becoming obedient to death—
>   even death on a cross!
> Therefore God exalted him to the highest place
> and gave him the name that is above every name,
> that at the name of Jesus every knee should bow,
> in heaven and on earth and under the earth,
> and every tongue acknowledge that Jesus Christ is Lord,
> to the glory of God the Father.

There are some complicated theological things going on in here. What does it mean that Christ emptied himself (a better translation than "made himself nothing")? He emptied himself of what? We don't quite believe that he emptied himself of deity, right? It seems to me that he empties himself of the prerogatives of deity. He gives up the advantages of his divine place, and takes on human likeness, which would have been something of a comedown for a member of the Trinity. One writer has described this as downward mobility.

Paul's not just rhapsodizing about this. "Your attitude should be the same as that of Christ Jesus." What Paul is trying to do here is solve a problem, and we do not find out what the problem is until the end of the epistle. He gives us the solution first and then he gives us the problem. It's Paul's version of "Jeopardy." Here's the answer, now what's the question? If you look at 4:2, you find the question: "I plead with Euodia and I plead with Syntyche to be of the same mind in the Lord."

That doesn't sound like much until you start thinking about it. I am convinced it is absolutely impossible to read the Bible well unless you can read it with some imagination. Imagine that you are the church to which this letter has been written and you don't all have a copy of it. I have the only copy and so I'm reading it to the church: "Have this mind in you which is also in Christ Jesus, who did not count equality with God as something to be greedily held on to but emptied himself and took on human nature, the nature of a servant, and became obedient to death even death on a cross." You're saying, "Yes! Amen! Rock and roll with that." And then a little later you hear "and I plead with you Euodia" (and Euodia may have been dozing at that moment but her head's popped up now) "and I plead with Syntyche" (and she may not have been with it up to this point but I got her attention now, and they are sitting on opposite sides of the building). Whatever it is between Euodia and Syntyche has become serious enough that Paul is calling them out in front of the whole church.

If two old sisters in a church get out of sorts with each other, that thing can get out of hand. Folks can pick a side, start to clump up, and you have competing fellowship groups (not to be confused with cliques, because this is a church). Now how can Paul solve this problem? Well, he already has. Talk about using a bazooka to kill a flea! "Have this mind in you which was also in Christ Jesus, who did not count equality with God as something to be greedily held on to but emptied himself, took on human nature in the form of a servant, and became obedient to death even death on a cross." If Euodia and Syntyche will live out the values of Jesus in this case, the problem will be solved.

So the story of Jesus that he's telling them is not just beautiful, it's functional. He's telling them to take on the life of Jesus and lay down their lives before one another rather than trying to protect their prerogatives and their turf. What's really interesting is that Paul doesn't say a thing about whether Euodia or Syntyche is right. The issue here is, "Will we live the story?" And the story is one of humbling ourselves. All of a sudden that beautiful passage just becomes troubling, because Paul actually expects us to live out the gospel of Jesus Christ in our lives, which will involve humbling ourselves before one another.

Learning Obedience

Let's go to a book that I'm really uncomfortable with: Hebrews. There are some great lines in here, so let me hit you with this one: "During the days of Jesus' life on earth, he offered up prayers and petitions with fervent cries and tears to the one who could save him from death, and he was heard because of his reverent submission" (Heb. 5:7). Isn't that odd? For one thing, he's appealing to the one who could save him, which seemed to suggest that Jesus couldn't save himself. "And he was heard because of his reverent submission." I may not remember that story very well, but it seems to me that he died. Isn't that the way you remember it? Is this a passage about the resurrection, because God saves him from death through the resurrection of the dead? I don't know. It's interesting to think about, isn't it?

But that's not the part of the passage I'm interested in. "Although he was a Son he *learned* obedience . . . ." Let's pause there for a moment. Jesus, all knowing, all perfect, God's Son, divine, *learns*. What does he learn? He learns obedience. As I start to reflect on that, it starts to make sense to me. Obedience is one of those things which you can only learn by experience. Think about being theoretically obedient. There is no theoretical obedience. There is only obedience, and I am not impressed by theoretical obedience.

Let me go back to Jesus' life and see if I can think this through a little more. Remember Jesus and the rich young ruler? The rich young ruler is a pretty good guy. I mean, he says he's kept the commandments. Pretty good guy. Jesus says, "You only lack one thing. Go sell all that you have, give it to the poor and come and follow me." Okay, he's not quite ready to go there. It's a bothersome passage, because I have to ask, What does that mean to me? Churches never like this story. From the very beginning the churches tried to find ways to not take this story seriously. A fine early Christian writer, Clement, who was rich and sophisticated, says, by the time he gets through with this story, that it really means that we are supposed to be rich in good deeds and poor in unrighteousness—but you can keep your stuff.

Or in the Middle Ages they take Jesus' statement, "It is easier for a camel to go through the eye of a needle than for a rich person to get into heaven" and turn "the eye of the needle" into a narrow gate in Jerusalem. If you go to Jerusalem now, they'll show you that gate and say, "This is the eye of the needle, and if you get a camel lined up just right you can get him through there; but it's pretty hard." But there's no evidence that there was any gate called "the eye of the needle" in Jesus' time. It appears that what he was talking about was a needle. It *is* hard to get a camel through a needle. It's not impossible, it's just hard. The key is getting the camel going the speed of light. At that point the camel liquefies and you can get it through, but you might not want to get on a camel going that fast.

If Jesus called upon me to sell all that I have and give it to the poor, would I? Of course, I can say "Yes" as long as he doesn't ask. You actually don't find out whether you're obedient or not until you've obeyed. You learn it by experience, and this text says that even Jesus was like that. He learned obedience. How? From what he suffered.

I teach introduction to philosophy, and it's a lot of fun. We cover the waterfront on philosophical topics. We do philosophy of religion, epistemology, and ethics. We address free will and determinism. We even do aesthetics. What is art? What is beauty? And we explore the problem of evil and suffering. How can you believe in an all-loving, all-powerful God in a world with so much suffering? I always start out this conversation by picking a student and saying, "If you had the power, would you do away with childhood leukemia? If you could snap your fingers and make sure that no baby would ever die again of leukemia, wouldn't you do that?" They always say yes, and who wouldn't say yes to that. And I say, "Well, do you think God's got the power to do that?" "Yes." "Then why doesn't he? Are you a nicer person than God is? You're willing to do it, but God isn't?"

It's tough. But even though it is impossible to explain every individual piece of suffering in the world, I want them to come away with the notion that the world is a better place because of the suffering that's in it. That's because things are learned in suffering that can be learned no other way. I'll grant you that, if God created the world to be Disneyland, he has done a dismal job. But what if this world was created to be a place where we could learn to be children of God and brothers and sisters to our fellow human beings. Then all of a sudden suffering has a role that is important.

What would we lose if we lost all suffering in the world? There's no longer any courage. There's no longer any compassion. There's no one to be compassionate towards. There's no longer any patience. There's no longer any endurance. There's no longer the love that doesn't give up when life goes badly. I don't know about you, but it sounds like you give up an awful lot. Suffering does humble us and teach us things that can't be learned any other way. And if the Hebrews writer is to be believed, Jesus goes through the human experience and learns obedience through suffering and thereby (in the writer's words) "becomes the author and finisher of our faith."

Living Outside the Camp

Let me look at my favorite passage in Hebrews 13. Those of you who have read Hebrews will know that there are a series of hortatory passages, that is, passages which say, "let us." There's a whole series of "let us" passages in Hebrews. You remember those? Okay, the last one in Hebrews 13 is the strangest of them all: "The high priest carries the blood of animals into the Most Holy Place as a sin offering, but the bodies are burned outside the camp. And so Jesus also suffered outside the city gate to make the people holy through his own blood. Let us, then, go to him outside the camp, bearing the disgrace he bore. For here we do not have an enduring city, but we are looking for the city that is to come" (Hebrews 13:11-14).

What does it mean to "go to him outside the camp, bearing the disgrace he bore"? We have Old Testament images of outside the camp. In the immediate context, the city that he's talking about is Jerusalem. A good bit in Hebrews suggests that some people are getting weary of the Christian thing and are thinking about sliding back into Judaism. So the writer often says, "Okay, don't give up, keep moving, keep moving forward." So he's trying to tell them, Don't retreat back into what is safe and secure, because where you're going to find Jesus is the place of disgrace and insecurity outside the camp.

It's just possible that when we're looking for Jesus we're often looking in the wrong places. We're looking on the inside, but where he is to be found is outside the camp where we bear his disgrace. And the reason you do this is in verse fourteen: "For here we do not have an enduring city, but we are looking for the city that is to come." The reason we go to Jesus in that insecure place is because all the places here that promise security are lying. There is no safe place. There is no safe religion. There is no safe church. There is no financial stability. There is no health plan that is safe. So here you don't have a city, so what are you going to do? You follow Jesus, believing that he will take you home. It's just that the route he takes you on is outside those sources of security, and it is going to be humiliating and disgraceful.

That's interesting. I am a voracious reader and I almost never get around to reading anything in my field—which explains a lot about my stalled career. I just read a book that bothered the daylights out of me. The book is *The Black Swan: The Impact of the Highly Improbable*. The premise of the book caught me. The author argues that most of the models of prediction that we work with are useless because they assume a constancy of life that is not true. The most formative events in life are ones that never hit your radar screen. If you're a financial investor, this book will drive you nuts. One of the things he points out is that the Nobel Prize committee continues to give prizes in economics to people whose theories have absolutely no grounding in reality. That's fascinating. There's no evidence that there's any validity to any of it at all. No real world evidence.

But my favorite story in the book is when the author does risk assessment for a casino in Las Vegas. If you are in the casino business in Vegas, risk assessment is really important because you want to make sure somebody is not going to come up with a betting scheme that will break the house. You can't afford that even once, so security is very important. He says what was interesting is that the casino never discussed what turned out to be their greatest risk. They never discussed what would happen if one of their star performers mauled their other star performer. They never discussed what would happen if the tiger attacked its master, which, if you'll remember, is what happened. It cost them millions. They didn't discuss that one because it wasn't on their radar screen.

The author says there are some grey swans out there, that is, unpredictable events that maybe you can catch. But he says that most of the most traumatic events are stuff that you cannot see coming. He's got no patience, for instance, with those who talk about the fact that the 9-11 events were predictable. He says of course they were predictable when you look at them after they happened. He says that is a lot like looking at a puddle and trying to figure out what the ice cube looked like before it melted. It is really hard to do.

And that really got me to thinking about the way I train students. Because the most formative events in their lives are going to be ones that they probably never see coming. About the best thing I can do is to try to spiritually form them in such deep ways that even when the tiger attacks they can survive. I don't know much else to do, but then it gets me thinking about this passage. If you plant yourself in the city that you think is secure, the tiger is going to get you every time.

So what do you do? Do you give up those sources of security and just follow Jesus to the place outside the city, bearing the disgrace he bore, because you don't have a city here? What does that have to do with humility? Well, it is an important reminder that many of the most important events in your life are going to be ones over which not only do you have no control but which you're not even going to see coming. And there is nothing like one of those events to burst your illusion about being one of those people who've got things under control. Nobody expects that their children will die before them. No one looks for that debilitating disease.

When we train our students to work in churches, we don't even attempt to cover every eventuality because the most informative event in the life of their church is something we will never see coming. Nobody expects that one of your leaders will be caught in a sexual molestation case. So we better take a much more humble stance towards life. We're not in control. The other thing we ought to do is be deeply suspicious of those who claim they are and not get pushed around by them. Because the society and the culture is going to say your worth and status is found in things that can disappear in a moment. We better find our identity somewhere else, because here we don't have a lasting city. The culture will push us towards taking a non-humble stance.

As I watch commercials with this perspective, it is fascinating. They perpetuate this illusion about the way life is going to be conducted. And so after all this, I'm coming to what is an utterly mundane conclusion. Let's be humble the way Jesus was. Let's don't claim our identity or our status based on passing things. Let's give up our prerogatives and lay down our lives and go outside the city gates and bear the disgrace he bore.

Among other things, that is a great stance from which to do evangelism. I mean, all these people out there are thinking, "Man, I've got to find some security in this very insecure world." We don't have any business offering that to them. We can offer you some security beyond this very insecure world. We can offer you a way to live in the midst of an insecure world, but you should know, if you join our church there's probably some bad stuff that's going to happen to you, because it happens to people here all the time. We can give you some ballast. We can give you a way to move on when that tiger you didn't see coming attacks you.

If we took this more humble stance towards the world, we might get a little better hearing for the gospel. I confess that I'm not very good at this. I'm struck with how few passages in Scripture I can preach with any credibility. In adopting the humble stance of Jesus, I just don't feel as if I have much credibility. And I want to invite ministers and church leaders to join me in a quest. In my more arrogant moments I think I'm a good teacher and a fair preacher, but I know what I really need to do for the next twenty years is become a better man, so that I will be able to speak the word that is before me with a little more credibility. Fools with tools are still fools. You know, it wouldn't do for us to have the best tools in the world and not be the people that God has called us to be. Which is to say that spiritual formation, formation in the image of Christ, trying to live out Christ's attitude and demeanor in the world, that's job one.

CHAPTER 8

WHAT I'VE LEARNED FROM THREE MONASTICS

I bought a table at a local furniture store. I really liked it. I thought I could squeeze it into the back seat of my car and take it home. The salesman says, "Great! We got one in the back for you." He comes out carrying a box. I said, "Do I have to put this together?" And he says, "Yes, but there's nothing to it. There are instructions in there."

So I get it home and the instructions might as well have been written in Russian. There was no way that anybody who didn't know how to put a table together would be able to with those instructions. So having pronounced an imprecatory psalm on the writer of those directions, I called the guy back and said, "You know, the reason I bought a table from you is because I didn't have the skill to build one." And he says, "Well, come back to the store and we'll give you one that's put together."

At that point I decided I have a great appreciation for people who can tell you how to do something in a way you can understand it. I teach biomedical ethics with Jim Nichols. I managed to get through high school and college without having a single competent science teacher. The result of that is I have always had a strong disregard for science. The only thing I got out of high school chemistry was a hole in my jeans, because I wasn't as careful with the chemicals as I should have been. But I have learned more science in teaching biomedical ethics with Jim than I learned in all my high school and college science classes.

So I want to introduce you to three people who have really helped explain things to me. They're mystics and the reason I like them is that there are things in my life I didn't understand and they were able to explain them to me. Like the guy who can write directions that can help you actually put a table together and a guy who can teach science so you can actually understand it, these are people who say things about your life that actually make sense of what you're going through.

St. John of the Cross

My friend St. John of the Cross explains some things that some of us really need help with. We get to a time in our lives, if we're serious about our Christianity, when a lot of stuff that we were deeply invested in doesn't matter to us so much anymore. Maybe we were pretty successful in business. Maybe we made some money and we've got a lot of nice things, but when we look around we're at that point in our lives where we realize they have to be dusted, and it just doesn't seem that important anymore.

There was that time in our lives where the next thrill was the most important thing. Maybe we were adventurers—I've enjoyed doing a few adventuresome things. I may not be quite over that yet, but I'm well on the way. Now those things don't excite us as much as they once did. And we might think that is a sign of spiritual maturity but then something really scary happens. The spiritual things that meant so much to us start to seem less and less important too. We go to church, But we can't figure out what we're doing there. We think, "This is a pretty nice group of people. I don't mind spending a little time with them, but if I sing that song one more time, I'll explode. Didn't that guy pray that same prayer last week? And I know he's preaching a different text, but boy that sure sounds like the same old sermon. And don't we need a little update on the Bible, I mean, I've read all of this one and I keep reading it and it's sounding pretty much the same."

Just as we lose interest in those other things, we lose interest in spiritual things. Unless we have a teacher like St. John of the Cross, we may think we are losing our faith. But St. John of the Cross has a different idea about that. Having personally walked through what he describes, I've decided that he's right. He calls it "the dark night of the soul." This much-abused term has been used to describe everything from the blues to really losing your faith, but John says the dark night of the soul is the way God prepares you for him and for eternity. He says that what God has to do is make you dissatisfied with everything in life, including your spiritual life, so you will reach for the only thing left, which is God.

So those things that meant so much to you and gave you such spiritual life become less and less important. As you start reaching around trying to find something else, John says, "Okay, now you're ready. There's one thing left. God."

Very early in my career I wrote a book well before I was ready to. And the book was roundly criticized. I guess that's something of a compliment. But I was too immature to have written such a book, so I went to somebody a lot older and wiser and said, "You know, I don't really like this criticism. This isn't what I signed up for. The problem with Christians is we are all here in a little huddle and the reason we're afraid to get out of our huddle is we're afraid if we do somebody on our own team will tackle us. I don't mind opposition from the powers of darkness, but I didn't sign up to have my own team tackle me."

And this wise, gentle person said, "Randy, you are not ready for this yet. You're not spiritually ready for this. Because there is a relationship with God that is so deep that if the church and your family and your friends all fell away, God would still be enough. Until you're ready to do that, you shouldn't be writing stuff like this." He was right.

John of the Cross says that when we give up on all those other things that give us meaning and life, when all around us is darkness, it is a really unpleasant experience. It's not a bad experience; it's just an unpleasant one. Because at the end of the way, he says, there is deep silence. And in that silence you find God. In the great line of the classic hymn, we find "the silence of eternity interpreted by love." We find in the midst of the darkness, in the midst of the silence, in the midst of the nothing, is a God who loves us so relentlessly that nothing else seems worthy in comparison.

I tried to follow John down this path and it's really difficult. The hardest part to believe is this: after you've totally emptied the room and closed your eyes and found your God, John says, when you open your eyes again, what you discover is that the room is full. Family and work and church are brought back in again, but they're brought back in a different way, because you know if they all fall away, that's okay because you still have God. You love those things now in the right way instead of the wrong way. You love them in a way that you don't have to own them or possess them. You love them but you know that if they all fell away it would be all right because you still have God.

When I do what John calls contemplative prayer I try to get quiet before God and say to God, "I don't have any agenda. I don't have any demands. I don't have any expectations. I'm not asking you to heal anybody. I'm not asking you to fix any problems. I'm not asking you to give me anything. I'm not even spending my time thanking you for anything. I'm not in adoration mode. What I'm wanting to do, God, is just sit here and be with the one I love because that's enough. And if there was nothing else in the world besides sitting here with you, that would be enough."

When I describe that, people often say, "Well, how do you know if you're praying or if you're just sitting?" My answer is, "I don't guess I do." And the next question is always. "Well, what are you doing?" And that one I do have the answer for: I'm preparing for eternity. I'm preparing for that time Paul describes when everything else falls away and there's nothing left but God. Let's hear that passage again from the first great Christian mystic:

> But we have this treasure in jars of clay to show that this all-surpassing power is from God and not from us. We are hard pressed on every side, but not crushed; perplexed, but not in despair; persecuted, but not abandoned; struck down, but not destroyed. We always carry around in our body the death of Jesus, so that the life of Jesus may also be revealed in our body. For we who are alive are always being given over to death for Jesus' sake, so that his life may also be revealed in our mortal body. So then, death is at work in us, but life is at work in you.
>
> Therefore we do not lose heart. Though outwardly we are wasting away, yet inwardly we are being renewed day by day. For our light and momentary troubles are achieving for us an eternal glory that far outweighs them all. So we fix our eyes not on what is seen, but on what is unseen, since what is seen is temporary, but what is unseen is eternal. (2 Corinthians 4:7-12, 16-18)

For those of you who have joined me in the process of wasting away as the things that we care most about fall away, we have Paul's reassurances, and we have the wise John of the Cross's reassurance: there's one thing left standing and that's God, and guess what?—that's enough. And it does strike me that trying to explain what it feels like to lose all interest in spiritual things because God is trying to draw you into loving him and him alone is impossible until you've lived through part of it. But when you've lived through part of it, it is wonderful to have somebody come in and say, "Oh no, that's not about losing your faith. That's about learning to love God and God alone with your whole heart. And that may be an unpleasant thing, but it's really good."

St. Francis of Assisi

Having talked about the person whose writings have had a greater influence on me than any other non-inspired writer, St. John of the Cross, I want to talk about the guy who wrote almost nothing. I take great heart in this, given my own dismal publishing record. Socrates and Jesus couldn't have gotten tenure either and neither could the mystic St. Francis of Assisi, who wrote very little. St. Francis, as far as I can tell, was a nut. But he was God's nut, which makes him a really interesting variety.

The stories about him are outrageous. The birds listen to him preach. He corrects a wolf on the error of his ways and creates peace. There are a few churches I'd like to send St. Francis to and see if he can pull that off with people. Near the end of his life he had the stigmata, the marks of Jesus, on his body. They're just astounding stories and through the years St. Francis has had enormous impact on the world and great impact on me. My assistant, Clint, was telling me about watching one of these programs showing the houses of some rich and famous people. One was a multi-million dollar house with a statue of St. Francis in the garden. It just proves irony is not dead in this world because, as you know, Francis would be a little uncomfortable in that setting.

I want to share three things that Francis has taught me. The first is simplicity and poverty. When he was young he was a bit of a hell raiser, and wound up giving up everything and became a beggar for Jesus. A lot of joking aside about the way I dress, I dress the way I do largely because of St. Francis. I'm trying to find all the ways I can to make my life more simple. Do I really need all the clothes in my closet? Do I really need all the dishes in my cabinet? Do I really need all the books on my shelves? Do I really need all the money in my wallet? I continue to be convicted by his willingness to give up all things for the sake of the Jesus that he calls Lord. I think we're all drawn to that example.

One of my favorite stories surrounding Francis has to do with Claire, who was the female side of this man/woman team in the same way that Teresa is kind of John of the Cross's counterpart. Claire and her spiritual sisters gathered up a little cloth and sold it to get a few things together to take to the lepers. Francis and Claire ministered to lepers when no one else wanted to. The story is that Claire and these ladies washed the skin of the lepers and then took the water with that dried up skin in it and drank it to have communion with the lepers. They had a willingness to give up all things in their compassion for other people.

I was with a group of Franciscans one summer and they said that to be a Franciscan you must make three commitments. The big Franciscan three. Chastity. Okay, I'm with you so far. Obedience. That's going to be a problem. Poverty. I think, I don't know how to do poverty. But I'm challenged to think about what it would mean in a responsible way to accept Francis' call to poverty.

Second, Francis has taught me to see God in creation. I am moved by Francis' ability to see God in all creation, especially in animals. Not only has he shaped the way I dress, he was largely responsible for me getting a dog. I was not particularly loving and I read about St. Francis and I thought if I could learn to love an animal, I might be able to work up to people. So I went in search of an animal I could love and wound up with Proko, the pug, who at our first meeting ran up and bit me on the toe. I was smitten. I believe , as we have gotten more separated from the land, from creation, and from the animal world, we have become more separated from God.

But these first two things aren't what most impressed me about St. Francis. I'm moved by those things and they've become part of my life, but what impressed me most about St. Francis is his joy. He is the mystic of pure, unmitigated joy. That always seemed so strange because he's a beggar. He's got nothing. He's out there wandering on the roads but you have these stories about this crazy beggar and his unbridled joy. Sometimes he'd be so overcome, he would start singing and dancing on the path and celebrating with whoever was there. I wonder what it is that makes a person find such joy in God?

Sometimes I think I can follow Francis down the path. I can get rid of some of my stuff, to be sure. I can start to practice some solitude and some silence. I can learn something about chastity and obedience. But I have this feeling that while I'm doing that I'm going to be a little grouchy about it. But there's nothing like that in Francis. He's got this leaping, dancing, joyful heart, and every time I read about him that's what I most want. I want to know what it's like to be a contemplative, a mystic, and a beggar who is unabashedly joyful.

St. Francis suffered some in his life. He lost some of his faculties toward the end of his life. Sometimes things were rough out there on the road ministering to people. He talked a lot about suffering, and encouraged people to take on suffering as a way of learning about and loving God. But the man's no masochist. Even in the midst of that suffering he continues to find this incredible joy.

I have to believe that, like St. John of the Cross, when Francis gave up all things he found the one thing that was really meaningful. He found God. He doesn't appear to be afflicted by loneliness or despair. He is a singing and dancing beggar for God. He is, in a word, a nut. When I was living in Nashville there was a man in the neighborhood of our school whom we called "dancing man" because he walked the streets all the time and was always dancing to music that nobody but he could hear. Occasionally he would bark. He was clearly disconnected from the world, and every time I saw him I would think, "I bet that's what they thought about St. Francis. He's walking around and he's singing and he's dancing and he's a little bit crazy." And like dancing man, I think Francis could hear some music that most of us can't hear. The music of the spheres. The music of God that's found in all things, and it filled him with joy.

So I want to follow Francis down that path. I do not want to be a miserable mystic. I do not want to be one of those grimly obedient Christians. I do not want to simplify my life and get grouchy doing it. I want to find the joy of the Lord that Francis found. I don't think I'm quite there, but I'm a lot happier than I used to be. And I'm grateful to Francis for showing that the way of poverty, obedience, chastity, solitude, and prayer doesn't have to be grim. It could be a party if you learn to hear the music.

St. Therese of Lisieux

One of my teachers in the ministry of spiritual guidance was a nun named Rose Mary Dougherty. Rose Mary and I were talking about the fact that many nunneries are basically going out of business. I said, "Tell me what you think that's about." And she said, "Well, in today's world there are a lot more opportunities for women who want to go for God than there used to be. But in my day if you wanted to go for God, there was only one way to do it and that was to become a sister."

So I want to introduce you to a mystic at the end of the nineteenth century who was a woman who decided to go for God. She's really unusual. Her name was Therese of Lisieux and she died of tuberculosis at the ripe old age of twenty four. She entered the monastery when she was sixteen and died eight years later.

I wanted to close with her for a couple of reasons. If St. John of the Cross and St. Francis of Assisi were in your living room, you would be intimidated. St. Francis would make you feel bad about all your stuff, and St. John would make you feel bad for breathing the same air that he does. They are giants. And they also lived back in the Middle Ages, while Therese died in 1897. So she's a little more modern, and she's as close as you'll ever come in a mystic to a nobody. That's the way she thought of herself.

She didn't ever do anything spectacular, but she is a great representative of women in Christian history. Even though you can find almost no women in the theological tradition, they are all over the spiritual and mystical tradition. Julian of Norwich and Teresa of Avila and St. Claire and Hildegard of Bingen—they're just everywhere.

She had it great growing up. Her parents really loved her. Her mother did die early, so Therese went to the monastery and fell passionately and madly in love with God and maintained that fierce love all of her short life. Almost nobody knew who she was when she died. She got famous afterwards, primarily because of the publication of her autobiography. Even though she considered herself a nobody, I guess we must give her credit for a little hubris, because at the age of twenty-four she had written her autobiography. I certainly didn't have one at the age of twenty-four; I don't think my life had even started yet.

Her little book, *The Story of a Soul,* is one of the most beautiful and accessible books ever written by any of the Christian mystics. I have no idea how many hundreds of thousands of people have read *The Story of a Soul,* but I'm guessing that many more than have read John of the Cross. You admire John, but read you read Therese.

Let me offer two or three things that we might learn from Therese. First, she shows us that a deep and passionate relationship with God is for plain old folks like us. We sometimes get the idea that to have a genuine and deep and powerful relationship with God you've got to be somebody special. Therese is really our living room saint, an ordinary person. What I admire most about Therese is her incredible commitment. She's in the monastery for over eight hard years. She took her vows very seriously and she's in a strict group and she went beyond what she had to do. It was a hard life.

One of the interesting things one learns from her spiritual autobiography is that God didn't deal with her particularly kindly during those eight years. We think of these mystics and saints as having a spectacular experience of God every day, but she didn't really have much of anything for eight years. She's just slugging away, loving God. She's what I'd call tough. This little slip of a girl was tough. She just kept at it and kept at it. She's one of those people who, when you look at her, makes you feel like a wuss. I don't want to be overly critical, but I think we have a lot of wussy Christians in the world. We demand immediate satisfaction. I want to have an experience now and I want God to show up when I want him to show up and I want him to show up how I want him to show up and if he doesn't do that, then I'll show him. I'll just take my marbles and go home.

Here's this young woman who year after year conscientiously serves God. Well, there's probably a lesson from that. We're all going to have spiritual dry periods. When I was out with some hermits I was complaining about having a bad week and they laughed at me. They said, "We had that spiritually dry period for years back there." The question is, "Are you in it for the long haul and do you believe that God can be faithful in the dry periods as well as other times?"

Second, Therese's life shows us how to love and serve people who are difficult to love. I really admire this about Therese, because I do not have this characteristic at all. If she's got any claims to being a saint, I think this is it. To be a canonized saint in the Catholic Church you have to have established miracles. Frankly, it is pretty hard to get her miracles off the ground. I don't think she's got the miracles to get in the hall of fame. But what she did is befriend the crankiest sisters in the order. Think about sisters in the order and all of the things that can happen to make them cranky, then multiply that by about twenty years, and then think about becoming that person's friend. Sainthood? Yes! In a world where we choose people for how they make us feel or what they can do for us or who are special friends to us, Therese sought to be a friend to those who most needed it. That was just the way of her life.

What would happen if all of us would give that much of our lives trying to be a friend to those who don't do very well with friends? One of the other things I really admire about Therese is that she was one of those people who doesn't mind accepting abuse. It's not that she's a masochist or wants to be a victim, it's that she wants to follow Jesus. She was working with this one cranky sister in the laundry who would keep throwing dirty laundry water in her face. She would do that all the time. If it was me, I think I'd whack that sister. I think there would be some ways to kind of straighten that out. But Therese was just not built that way. She understood that God redeems the world by self-giving love. It's not victimization. It's not abuse. It's just that she is not going to allow herself to be driven off from people who need the love of God. I admire that very much.

I had a student assigned to me. I think it was part of his penance. Exactly what I had done is not clear to me, but it became part of mine too. If he thought you were getting close, he would figure out a way to drive you away. He would not let you get close. I've got to admit, I'm not as good at this as Therese was. I was a little easier to push off than I should have been. Therese had the attitude, "It doesn't matter how hard you try to push me away, I'm just going to keep loving you; so you might as well get used to it, because that's the way it's going to be." Here are a few of her own words: "I am a little brush which Jesus has chosen in order to paint his own image in the souls he entrusted to my care, humble, loving child."

I hope some of you might be inspired to read *The Story of a Soul,* but I hope even more you'll be moved to develop your own relationship with God that is as deep and profound as she had, knowing that it's for ordinary people. I especially want to speak that word to women as we continue to struggle with the relationship between men and women. I think of the wise women who have changed my life. I think about Rose Mary Daugherty, who helped lead me into the ministry of spiritual guidance. I think of the woman at the Donelson Church where I preached for ten years. When people were struggling with the spiritual life, she was the one I would send them to, because her life was the epitome of amazing grace. Whether it was male or female who needed spiritual help, no one could come within her grasp without being deeply and profoundly changed.

In the tradition where women found no place in theology, they found a deep place in spirituality and the ministry of spiritual guidance. While we're trying to work all the complicated stuff out, I just want us to look around for the saints and mystics around us, male and female, who serve quietly and passionately and lovingly out of their relationship with God. We can't afford to be half a church. We just can't.

CHAPTER NINE

FOUR WAYS OF PRAYING

I t is intimidating to talk about prayer because I don't have any credibility with you, and prayer is a deeply personal, though not private, interaction with God. I did part of my growing up in Salina, Kansas, and I went to Salina a few years ago to perform an unusual act. I performed the wedding ceremony for my father. My mother died a few years ago of a brain tumor, and my father developed a romance with an old family friend. I then had to do what no boy should ever have to do: watch his father date.

After this gruesome exhibition, they decided they wanted to get married. They then asked me to perform the ceremony. I didn't know what to do. What do you do when you're marrying your father? I didn't even know what to say. Do you say, "Do you, Dad, take you, Melba?" That didn't sound right. So anyway, there I am. I'm performing the ceremony for these two people who both had more than thirty-five years of wonderful marriages, so I just skipped the sermon part and went straight to the "I do's." That just seemed like the safest thing to do.

Afterwards my Dad says, "Randy, what happened to the sermon there?" I said, "Well, Dad, you know I just didn't feel as if I had any credibility in that area with you." He says, "Randy, you're my son. You don't have any credibility with me in any area."

That's the way I feel when I talk about prayer. Not sure I have any credibility. But I have spent time with those who do. I spent forty days with hermits in the wilderness, hermits who spend their life in prayer. Here are some of the things I learned from them.

When you start talking about the "how to's" of prayer, it's always worrisome because you may make it more difficult than it needs to be. When I was out at the hermit's community, one of the things they taught me (by the way it's not easy to get a hermit to teach you anything; it's more difficult to get information out of a hermit than it is a spy) is that you should not pray the way you think you should, you pray the way you can and God honors that. And so I want that to keep reverberating through your head. If some of the ways of praying that I talk about don't appeal to you, if God doesn't seem to be calling you to those, then don't pray the way you think you should, pray the way you can and God will honor that.

Praying is about entering into the divine reality and forming a deep relationship with God. I first want to reflect on some different ways of praying. This largely comes from the book *Armchair Mystic* by Mark Thibodeaux, who is a Roman Catholic. You'll quickly find, if you read that book, quite a few things you don't agree with. But it is a wonderful book on how to enter into contemplative prayer. He suggests there are four ways of praying—though I think there are five. So I'm going to talk about his four and then in the next chapter I'll talk about one more and about two special problems in prayer, intercessory prayer and unanswered prayer.

Saying Your Prayers

The first way of praying is is *talking at God*. And what he really means by this is rote prayer. Not wrote, but rote. The first way we learn to pray is by parroting, or mimicking, the prayers that we hear others say or that we are taught. For instance, one of the very first prayers most of us learn is "God is great, God is good, now we thank you for this food." Almost rhymes, doesn't it? Or the awful, "Now I lay me down to sleep. I pray the Lord my soul to keep. If I should die before I wake . . . ."

We first learn to pray by listening to other people. My friend, Mike Cope, was telling me that every time he gets up to preach at his church, he always prays that God will pour through him the gift of preaching. And so a preschooler from his church was praying over the hamburgers at home and you know what he prays, right? "God pour through me the gift of preaching." All he's doing is using the words that other people have given him. That's the way we first learn to pray.

In some ways, that is a childish way to pray. In other ways, it's simply a childlike way to pray that we really never outgrow. For instance, many of us still find praying the Lord's Prayer a deep and profound way to pray. In its simplicity, in its submission, in its openness to God, the Lord's Prayer continues to bless us in many ways. Another really powerful way of doing rote praying is praying the Psalms. The Psalms have for two thousand years been the prayer book of the church, and I continue to find praying the Psalms to be a wonderful way to pray.

So I want to suggest a little discipline to you. This will be the most important thing I say in this chapter. It will bless you more than anything else you could do. If you will read eighty verses of Psalms a day, you will get through the Psalter every month. In the monasteries they pray the whole Psalter every week. But they don't have a life. We've got things to do here, right? But you can read eighty verses of the Psalms in probably fifteen minutes. So in fifteen or twenty minutes a day, you'll get through the whole Psalter every month. There are about 2,400 verses in Psalms. In February you must put the pedal to the metal, but you get the idea.

Everybody who has taken the dare and prayed the eighty verses a day has found it to be an incredible blessing. Because what Psalms teaches us to do is to look at the world through the eyes of praise. What Psalms does is give us language for whatever is going on in our lives. There are times when I need to say things to God but I just don't have any words. My goal has been to become so familiar with the Psalms that, no matter what is going on in my life, I've got a psalm for it. And I'm getting there. So twelve times a year I'm all the way through the Psalms. And it's become part of the way I think and the way I live. When I have sin in my life and I need some confession, Psalm 51 or Psalm 39 come rushing in, and when God has totally abandoned me and there's no hope in sight, Psalm 88 becomes my friend.

I had this interesting experience. I was preaching through some Psalms. I don't do that very often because Psalms are notoriously difficult to preach. Preaching Psalms is like explaining a joke—if you have to explain the joke you've lost the impact of it. If you have to preach a psalm, then you really kill it because it's the poetry in the psalm that does the heavy lifting.

I had preached my way through a few psalms and a guy came up to me afterwards and said, "I want to share something with you. Years ago I went through a really deep and dark depression and it went on for some time. And I did commit myself to the Psalms." And he says, "I made a list of the good psalms and the bad psalms." And I said, "Well, that's really interesting. Tell me about it." And what was interesting is that, when he was in that depressed state, Psalm 23 wasn't a good psalm, it was a bad psalm, because, he said, it was too sweet, too optimistic for what he was experiencing. "When I read one of those really dark psalms," he said, "it ministered to me in a way that the happier psalms didn't." That's very counterintuitive to me. That's not what I would have thought of doing, but I think it is interesting how those different kinds of psalms seek us and find us in our different places in life if we'll commit ourselves to them.

I know a minister with whom I've never agreed. He would say, "It's 3:00 o'clock," and I'd say, "Prove it." It was a relationship like that. But from time to time I saw him go into a house of mourning and do nothing but open his Bible and start to read some psalms. Talk about powerful ministry! So this business of *talking at God* I take really seriously. I think rote prayers are extremely helpful and if you're one of those creative sorts, you may want to go outside of Scripture and not just have the Lord's Prayer and the Psalms but find all sorts of wonderful written prayers that minister to you.

Conversational Prayer

The second way of praying is *talking to God*. Thibodeaux says that at some point we get tired of using other's words because we have some things we want to say to God on our own. And so we quit talking *at* God and we start talking *to* God. This is the one I'm going to spend the least time on because this is the one that's most natural and the one we usually need less coaching on.

I do, from time to time, run into people who seem to have trouble talking with God. And I don't have a lot of suggestions to make about that. One of the things I would suggest, if you're having trouble talking with God, is to quit sitting and start walking, because sometimes walking and talking is a more natural thing to do. Or jog. I see joggers who look as if they're deep into it. I'm assuming they're praying and not just dying out there. It's hard to tell sometimes.

I tell people, if you have trouble just talking with God, to quit praying and start talking. Just forget all the formalities of prayer and just start talking with God and share whatever comes to mind. Just let it be free association. If that doesn't work, I say, "Okay, if you're having trouble talking to God, try this. Tell him a joke." And they say, "You've got to be kidding." I say, "No, no, no." And they say, "That's not going to work." And I say, "Why not?" And they say, "Well, God knows all the jokes." And I say, "Yeah, but it's all in how you tell it."

Of course, the point is just to cut yourself loose and open yourself up to being able to share whatever is on your mind with God, including your anger and your frustration and your disappointment. First of all, it's impossible to hide that stuff from God. Second, God can handle it. And if the Psalms teach us anything, it is that as we share that stuff with God, things happen. It's amazing how often in the Psalms you start out beating up on God but before you wind up, you're praising God. The reason I like that kind of praying is that it takes God seriously.

Some of us have such low expectations of God that it would be impossible for him to disappoint us. I think God would prefer we have high expectations and then get in a conversation with him about why things aren't going that way. Now, if you set up a picture of God that expects so little that you're never going to be disappointed, then your faith will never be troubled. The problem is you will cut yourself off from all of those wonderful relational moments that could happen.

One of the great joys of my life is getting to worship on a regular basis with college students, who continue to teach me about what it means to worship. They are so open to the worshipful moment that two things happen. One, they are easily distracted or disappointed when it doesn't go the way they think it ought to. But number two, they have those stunning experiences that those of us who aren't open to them never have.

I can still remember the day in one of my classes when I was trying to teach students that there were some good songs that were written more than five minutes ago. A contemporary song is one where the ink is still wet. My taste in church music is that I don't want to sing anything by a person who's not dead. And I don't want them freshly dead either. We were singing some songs about the holiness of God and we did some contemporary hymns and then I introduced them to the wonderful "Holy, Holy, Holy." I had lectured on the holiness of God and then we moved into a brief worship experience. We started singing "Holy, Holy, Holy," and I noticed this kid on the back row who drops to his knees, puts his nose on the floor, and sings, "Holy, Holy, Holy." And I'm thinking, "Boy, I wish I could do that. I wish I was so open to the worshipful moments that I just do what he does."

If we're willing to really open up in our talking with God, it will be lively. Sometimes you'll do some yelling and screaming. I remember one night I threw a rock at God. I think he threw it back. I'm trying to think how that worked out. God can handle it. If the Psalms teach us anything, it's that God can handle whatever you bring to him.

Listening to God

The third way of praying is *listening to God*. At some point we get tired of the one sidedness of the conversation, and so frequently we want to hear some things from God too. This is a little tougher for us. We often have problems with the notion of listening to God, but we shouldn't. I want to show you a couple of Old Testament passages that will help us see this. First, consider 1 Kings 18. Here we have the story of Elijah on Mt. Carmel. My favorite part comes in verse 26 and following, where we get a unique view into pagan worship. "They took the bull given them and prepared it. Then they called on the name of Baal from morning until noon. 'Oh Baal, answer us,' they shouted, but there was no response, no one answered, and they danced around the altar they had made. At noon Elijah began to taunt them."

This is really my favorite part because I'm a college professor. I occasionally find it necessary to taunt my students and I need a proof text, and this is the text that proves that some taunts are holy. So what do I say to students when they come to my office and say, "Why am I making an F in your class?" I say, "Because there's nothing lower." But it's a holy taunt. Or my new favorite: "You're depriving some village of an idiot."

Back to the text: "At noon Elijah began to taunt them. 'Shout louder,' he said. 'Surely he's a god. Perhaps he's deep in thought or busy or traveling, maybe he's sleeping and must be awakened.'" "So they shouted louder and slashed themselves with swords and spears as was their custom, until their blood flowed. Midday passed and they continued their frantic prophecy until the time for the evening sacrifice, but there was no response. No one answered. No one paid attention."

Okay, here you see what you do when you worship an idol. You yell, you dance, you slash, and you yell louder. And the reason you do all of that is because the idol is going to do exactly nothing. So any noise, any enthusiasm, any activity generated is going to be human because the idol is not going to do anything. I will resist the temptation at this point to go into a dissertation about worship renewal, which often looks to me to be profoundly pagan. A little more noise. A little more activity. A little more enthusiasm.

Compare this passage to Habakkuk 2, beginning with verse 18, where the prophet starts talking about idol worship and then winds up talking about the living God. "Of what value is an idol, since a man has carved it? Or an image that teaches lies? For he who makes it trusts in his own creation; he makes idols that cannot speak. Woe to him who says to wood, 'Come to life!' or to lifeless stone, 'Wake up!' Can it give guidance? It is covered with gold and silver; there is no breath in it. But the Lord is in his holy temple; let all the earth keep silence before him."

Habakkuk says that when you worship the living God the first act of worship is silence, because he's alive and he's at home and he might actually have something to say. Listening prayer presumes there is a living God who wishes to be in relationship with us. As you do some praying there will be periods of silence and that silence won't be empty. It will be full of the presence of God. As the Psalmist says, "Be still and know that I am God."

God has never been prone to give me all of the information I want whenever I want it. God doesn't, in those moments of silence, stand at my shoulder and speak in my ear what I should do. But I do believe that if we take a listening stance towards God, he will guide us into deeper relationship and wisdom. That's what you would expect from a living God who comes to meet us in prayer.

One of things we need to learn to do is pray Scripture. Scripture needs to be a two-way communication with God. One of the ways that Scripture really comes alive for us is when we develop a listening stance towards it. Our Bible reading isn't always as transforming as it should be because, instead of allowing the Bible to interrogate us, we interrogate the Bible. And you don't call Scripture into question. Scripture calls you into question. If you develop this listening posture toward Scripture, then it will speak to you in transforming ways.

I have come to believe there is only one really serious Bible study question and that is, "If I took this text seriously, what would have to change?" And the most important Bible study skill is not learning to read Greek, although that is an important skill. The most important skill in studying Scripture is a willingness to listen, to allow Scripture to call us into question and to invite us into change. There are other ways of listening that I'm going to address, but let me get these different ways of praying out here first.

Being with God

The fourth way of praying is simply *being with God*. Eventually we get to the point where even all the talking and listening becomes too much and we just spend time with God. I have to tell you that this is

my favorite way of praying. I want you to think about the relationship in your human life that means the most to you. It will most
likely be the relationship with your spouse. If you will think about
it, some of the most important and precious moments you have had
are when you weren't trying to accomplish anything together. You
didn't have an agenda. You weren't saying anything. You were simply
being there. You were just being with the one you love.

My favorite way of praying has become simply to be there with
God. Just to spend time with the one I love. I don't have an agenda. I
don't have any demands. I don't have any expectations. I tell God, "I
don't know what's going to happen here. Nothing needs to happen
here. I just want to be with you. I just want to give you my full and
undivided attention for this time we're together."

It's almost impossible to talk about this without running
through your own experience and so let me tell you about my own
journey. You can bounce it off your own. A few years ago I was
going through what I now know would be described as the dark
night of the soul. What I thought was going on at the time was that
I was having a mid-life crisis. I had a wonderful ministry going at
my university in Nashville, and things had never gone better at the
Donelson Church where I was ministering. But I had this restless-
ness of heart that I could not get rid of. I felt as if there was something else I was supposed to do. I didn't know what was going on.

I tried to solve it in a variety of ways. What do you do when
you're having a mid-life crisis? Well, I didn't have a wife to divorce.
I was too uncoordinated to ride a motorcycle. So I moved to Texas.
But that did not solve the problem. The problem was, when I moved
to Texas, I went with me. That restless heart just came with me. I
had a great new ministry going at Abilene Christian University but
I was restless.

I conducted a retreat in the Corpus Christi area and met a
young man there interested in the traditional spiritual disciplines,

as I was, and so when I returned home he emailed me and said, "I just went to an interesting place to pray for a few days. I think you might find it interesting, too. Here's their website." And so I went to the website and it was basically the site of a small hermit community. Now, there's already something wrong with this: hermits with a website—what is the world coming to? And these three hermits were living together—that didn't seem right. I mean, they should be out by themselves, but I guess hermits have to live somewhere.

On the website I saw that they had a program called a "forty-day wilderness experience" which is basically where you went for forty days of silent prayer. They would ask you to spend six hours a day for forty days praying. Just giving God your undivided attention. I could not get that out of my mind. I couldn't quite pull the trigger to go, but I couldn't get it out of my head either. And so I started taking little baby steps. I first cleared my schedule—not an easy thing to do. And then I sent in my application to see if they would allow me to come, but I still hadn't made the commitment because I hadn't put any money on the line.

I was thinking, "Okay, if I do this there are two things that can happen and they're both bad. One would be 'nothing' and the other would be 'something.'" If nothing happens, then that really raises questions about God and my faith. But if something happens, I'm not going to be in control of what happens and who knows how God's going to mess with me. So I finally pulled the trigger and decided to go, much to the surprise and wonderment of almost all my friends.

My family thinks I've lost my mind because their idea of praying is asking God for things and giving the whole grocery list. But you can do that in a day and then you have thirty-nine days left over. And I'm trying to explain, "I'm not going to do that. I'm just going to go out there and be with God and see what happens, see what he wants to do."

My friends started teasing me about what might happen. They would say, "You're going to get out there and God's going to tell you to get married." So I start praying, "Okay God, I'm going to go, just don't mess with me, please."

And then when it's time for me to go, my friends start worrying. They say, "What's going to happen if you're out there for twenty days and you're going crazy and you can't stand it anymore? What are you going to do?" And I said, 'Well, I'm going to pack up my car and come home." They said, "You can do that?" And I said, "It's a hermit's community, not a concentration camp." They seemed to have a picture of nuns with machine guns sitting on the barbed wire ready to mow you down if you decide to leave.

So off I go. I get down there to South Texas and it's hot and hermits don't have air conditioning. I live my life at a pretty rapid rate, like a lot of you do. The first experience there was just decompression. You're almost pacing the floor because you don't have anything to do. No television. No radio. No computer. No phone. They said you weren't supposed to bring your cell phone. I smuggled mine in, but there was no signal out there. I found that as you get closer to God, you seem to get further from civilization.

The first several days were an absolutely miserable experience. What happened to me is what happens to a lot of people when they do this. When I got quiet, with nobody but me and God, all of the sin and crud in my life came rushing to the surface. In my busyness with speaking and writing, I can usually keep that stuff pushed away. Like right now as I'm writing, I'm conveying the image of myself I want you to see. But when language is taken away from me, when an activity is taken away from me, and all I have is me and God's glory and holiness, then there's no place to hide.

Isaiah describes this experience in Isaiah 6. As the glory of the Lord appears all around him, what does Isaiah say? "Woe is me. I am undone. I am a man of unclean lips and I dwell in the midst of a people of unclean lips." There was stuff coming up that I didn't even know about. I'll give you one little glimpse; I can't tell you everything. You'll understand that, right? One of the things I came to see is how being the smartest kid in school had almost destroyed my spiritual life. When I was growing up I was the smartest kid in school. I made the best grades in all the classes. You can ask any of my classmates who Randy is and they will tell you: he's the smartest kid in school. But one of the things I discovered is that I had spent the rest of my life trying to be the smartest kid in school. And much of my worthiness before God was based on how productive I was being at any particular time. That will destroy your spiritual life. Because nobody is productive and successful all the time.

That was just one of the things. There was much darker stuff. And so I go to the hermit who is serving as my spiritual director and I say, "This is what's going on and I don't really like it. I don't know if it's coming from me or from God or from Satan, and I don't know what to do." He said, "Let's don't worry about where it's coming from now. Let's think about what to do with it." And he came up with just the right image. He said, "This is like smoke coming out of a chimney." He says, "If you want to you can try to cap the chimney, but all you're going to do is drive the smoke back down into the house. Which is what you've been doing your whole life. Or you could let it go."

That's a lot easier to say than it is to do. But there was a moment a little later on in that experience where I started to be able to let that stuff go; and I discovered the truth in my heart that I already knew with my head, which is, "God loves you just the way you are." And in that moment the verse of a hymn came to me—a verse of "Just As I Am" which we seldom sing: "Just as I am, thy love unknown has broken every barrier down."

What a moment! I have wished over and over again that I could package that up and give it to students who are racked by guilt and success anxiety, but I can't. You have to go get it. I want to tell you that, if you enter into this silent listening prayer, initially the experience may not be all that pleasant. But I want you to hear that the God who reveals is the God who heals. And if you stay around, there is something wonderful on the other side of that place. If you stick with it, you find that as God reveals the depths of sin in your heart, he then comes in and heals it. And the grace of God becomes not just a theory, but a reality. That's what happens when we start to listen.

Listening and Discernment

As you enter into this listening prayer and being with God, you are going to have all sorts of intuitions, urges, and feelings. Not all of those are the Holy Spirit. You have to be discerning. When you think that God is calling you to do something, one of the things you do is take it back to God in prayer. The other thing you do is open up to the community for their discernment too. That's why prayer is both a personal and a communal experience.

When I think God is calling me to do something other than what I'm doing, one of the first things I want to do is to gather four or five people around me who know me well, who love God deeply, and who love me. I'm going to say, "I think this is what God is calling me to do. I want you to start praying over this and I want us to see what we have here." Because I am so self absorbed, there is virtually nothing that I cannot talk myself into and make it turn into the will of God. And the only protection I have against that willfulness is the wisdom of the community. Continue to pray over it, offering it up to the community for discernment.

I love my students and we always have these lively conversations going which, if you didn't know us better, would look like arguments. But they're not. They're lively discussions. Sometimes they use language that gets under my skin, and when they do I point it out to them.

For instance, one that's become bothersome to me is, "The Lord laid it on my heart." If you use that language, I'm not really objecting to it. I use it occasionally myself. My problem is how glibly it's often said. "The Lord has laid on my heart" has become the ultimate trump card. I'll go to a place to preach and we have a worship program planned. I'll find out it's been completely changed because the Lord has laid on the heart of the worship leader to go in another direction. And all I can say is, "The Lord has laid on my heart that that was not the Lord who laid that on your heart."

I tell my students, "When I listen to what the Lord has laid on your heart, sometimes I'm beginning to think that the Lord is an idiot. What frustrates me is that God lays stuff on your heart when you're on the way from the gym to the cafeteria. And I spent a summer with three hermits out in the desert who have been there thirty-five years trying to discern the voice of God. And you've managed to be able to hear it on this little jaunt."

That doesn't mean God is never laying stuff on our hearts. It just means we've got to learn to listen and to be discerning. I'm absolutely convinced God is going to come in and lead you. You're going to take it up in prayer, and you're going to share it with one another, and you're going to become discerning about it.

So it turns out that God is not calling me to be a hermit. My prayer life is to be part of my ministry. It was getting close to my time to leave and I had all sorts of conflicting emotions. I was very anxious to go. I know that spending forty days praying sounds like a romantic idea, but I can tell you the reality is quite different. It's boring, it's grinding, it's hot, and the vast majority of the time you can't tell anything is happening. I was looking forward to being back with my church and my people and my students. I was looking forward to M & Ms, and getting reacquainted with my dogs. I was also thinking that when I get back home I will have a thousand e-mails waiting.

You learn a lot about yourself when you're in a place where you're not allowed to speak. We were only allowed to speak at Sunday lunch. The rest of the time we were silent and at Sunday lunch we could talk for an hour. I don't know if you've noticed, but I'm a really witty person. And often stuff would happen and I would have something very clever to say about it and I would not be allowed to say it until Sunday lunch. And by the time that hour came around, it just didn't matter anymore. It's pretty hard for a guy who makes his living with his tongue to find out that about ninety-five percent of what he says is totally unnecessary.

And then I leave and it's like the whole world is screaming. I was on a plane trip shortly after that and the three people sitting in front of me talked the whole time at the same time. This is such a noisy world. But there was this moment as I was getting ready to leave when I remember uttering a prayer to God because I felt so close and deeply in tune with him there. It's still a second home to me. I go back out there a couple of times a year for a few days. I said, "Okay, God. Will you come with me?" And it was as if all heaven and earth laughed. Not the make-fun-of-you laugh, but the big-hearted embracing laugh that said, "Do you really think I'd let you leave without me?"

CHAPTER TEN

WHEN LIFE BECOMES PRAYER

L et me return to where I started in the last chapter. One of the mistakes I've made in my ministry is trying to push people into new kinds of prayer before they are ready to go there. You don't pray the way you think you should, you pray the way you can and God honors it. But I particularly want to address those who are experiencing frustration or dissatisfaction with their prayer life. That could be for several reasons. One reason might be that your life has gotten out of sync with your prayer and when life and prayer aren't working together, it always creates tension.

Do you remember reading *Huckleberry Finn* your sophomore year in high school? Some of you are thinking, "I'm not sure it had been written when I was a sophomore in high school," but it was. It's the same sophomore year in high school you start off by reading *The Scarlet Letter*—which is a great disappointment, because it's supposed to be about sex, but it's still boring. Leave it to the Puritans to take a salacious topic and make it utterly boring. And then after that you read *Huckleberry Finn* and you're shocked because you didn't know it was literature—and a wonderful book. The second half is a bit of a mess, but you remember that the basic story centers around Huckleberry Finn who's sailing down the Mississippi River with a companion. The companion is the runaway slave, Jim. At one of the most gripping points in the book, Huckleberry Finn is having a crisis of conscience; he believes he should turn Jim in, because Jim's a runaway slave. So he decides to pray over it and he's trying to pray to God to give him the strength to turn Jim in, but it turns out he can't do it and his conclusion is this: "You can't pray a lie."

Dissatisfaction with Your Prayer Life

When people are troubled in their prayer lives, always the first thing I say is, "Okay, before we talk about your prayer life, let's talk about your life." When our prayer life breaks down, it's often because there's something that's gone haywire in our life more generally and that makes it very difficult to approach God with any authenticity.

That might be one reason. But the second reason we might experience dissatisfaction with our prayer life is that God is calling us to a deeper or different kind of prayer. We do not move in our spiritual lives until we experience some dissatisfaction with what we've got. That is a fundamental learning theory. To get people to learn new things or to do new things, they have to become dissatisfied with the way things are. I'm one of those people who frequently begins programs to improve my health, and they almost never go anywhere, because the plain fact of the matter is, I'm not dissatisfied enough yet to make it work. I don't have heart trouble. I don't have high blood pressure. There are people in shock who have higher blood pressure than I do. I'm not even trying to live to be ninety. Everybody on my dad's side of the family lives to be a hundred and twenty. But their minds all go about seventy. I'm trying to take such poor care of myself that everything will play out about the same time.

Some of you have made drastic changes in your life and in almost every case it was because there was something that motivated you to do that. Heart attack. Doctor telling you to improve your health or die. I've got a friend who is seventy years old, and we go online to check his health age. His health age is about fifty. My friend Ken is in his early forties. His health age is like twenty-five. He jogs like a hundred miles a day. My health age is dead.

So something has motivated you to make the change. God will sometimes create dissatisfaction with where you are to get you to move. So I don't want you to assume that just because you're having trouble in your prayer life that you're in the middle of a spiritual crisis. We do want to check your life first and see what's going on, but God may just be calling you to a deeper or different way of praying. Maybe you've just gotten tired of all this jabbering on and it's time to learn to listen in prayer. Or maybe God's calling you to the wonderful peace and quiet of just being there. This has become my favorite way of praying now. I'll take an hour out and do it every day. I'll say to God, "Okay, I'm going to be here for an hour. I don't have any expectations. I don't have any demands. I don't have an agenda. I'm just going to be here. I just want to be here with you." It's like an hour's vacation every day.

Intercessory Prayer

With very few exceptions I find I have very little to say in prayer anymore. When I do want to talk, it almost always has to do with intercessory prayer. I want to say first that intercessory prayer is for me a great mystery. It has always seemed odd to me that I would pray on behalf of somebody else. What do I expect to happen? But intercessory prayer is one of the kinds of spoken prayer that I find meaningful. In some ways it's gotten much simpler and in other ways it is still very complicated. One of the things I have found in intercessory prayer is that I almost never know what the person really needs. I can guess. I have my own notions, but a lot of times I just don't know what needs to happen.

So one of my favorite ways of doing intercessory prayer is simply to do visual prayer. Let me take you through a little exercise here. I want you to think about somebody you want to pray for, someone who's important to you. It may be a physical matter that's most on your mind and that's fine. My preference would be that you pray over a spiritual matter. And don't worry if that person has been resistant to all the praying that's been done for him or her. What I want you to do is just picture Jesus—however you picture him—walking up to that person and wrapping his arms around and just holding him or her. I don't know what that person you're praying about may need in particular, but I know whatever else she needs, she needs to be embraced by the love of Jesus Christ. And in this moment it's not yours to make that happen, it's just yours to offer up that picture to God and just hold it there.

As you do that, it's possible that God may call you to do something in reference to that person, but not necessarily. And if God is calling you to do something with regard to the person that you're holding before your eyes, I want you to be open to being moved by God to do that, because when we pray for a person we are tied to that person in deep and special ways. But it could be all that you're supposed to do is just pray for them. We're not doing anything but trying to join God in his great desire for that person to come into the arms of Jesus. And we pray this through Christ our Lord. Amen.

Maybe you'll make the commitment to do that a few minutes every day for the next thirty days. Just keep calling them back into the arms of Jesus. Whenever I do this, and it's frequently, I know there are always parents out there who are praying for children. They don't know how to pray or what to do, and when you don't know what to do, this is what you do. And you never give up. You never give up. You let God do what God will do.

Unceasing Prayer

Let me suggest one other way of praying. I have developed a great regard for monastic disciplines. I am a lay contemplative of Gethsemani monastery. All that means is, I try to live out the rule of St. Benedict in my ordinary life. That is, I try to live out the rules of simplicity and prayer in my daily life. The monks pray seven times a day. It starts with a 3:15 AM vigil. I always thought it was interesting that these monks get up in the middle of the night to pray that God will continue to watch over them and care for the world while the rest of us sleep. I don't know how you feel about that—I feel good about it. If you total up all the time they spend in prayer in those seven times of communal prayer, it adds up to about two and a half hours; and the rest of the time when they're not engaged in communal prayer, they're off somewhere praying alone. But again, they don't have a life. All they have to do is pray.

I have found that the discipline of praying seven times a day makes all the difference in the world. For me those prayers often don't last more than ninety seconds. There is great benefit in turning the eyes and the heart back to God for that brief period of time.

I've joked about how my freshman Bible majors one year did more for my prayer life than any group I have been around in a long time. They were the most immature group of people I had ever been around. They just drove me nuts. They would bring their toys to class. A hockey stick—why do you bring a hockey stick to Bible class? Soccer ball. Gorilla suit. Toys. So immature. And I found that what I needed to do every day before I went to class was go to my office and pray. I'd say, "Dear God, help me not to kill them today. God, this is the way you made them. This is where they are in life. Help me go in there and be Jesus to them today. Move them this far." And I cannot tell you how much difference that made. Ninety seconds transformed what happened over those next couple of hours. And so as I face the challenges of a typical day, I try to build in those sixty or ninety seconds of prayer just to remind myself of who I am.

Have you ever had the experience of just totally forgetting who you are? I had gone to a fast food restaurant. It was taking forever to get through the drive-thru. I don't know why they call them fast food restaurants. It took me twenty minutes to get up to the window to place my order and another ten or fifteen minutes to get around to pay. When I finally paid and the guy gave me my money back, I looked at it and said, "You've cheated me. You owe me one more dollar." And he says, "No, I don't think so." And I said, "Yeah, here's how much it cost. Here's how much I gave you. And this is what you gave me back. You owe me one dollar."

And he says, "Okay, wait a minute," and he disappears. He comes back and says, "I talked to the manager and we'll have to count the cashbox to be sure." I said, "Oh, forget it." I'm getting ready to drive out with my friend in the car and I looked over at him and I pull back out and I park the car and I say, "I want that dollar." At this point it has nothing to do with money. You understand that, right?

So we go into the restaurant and I'm sitting there looking impatient, patting my foot and the guy says, "Well, sorry I have to take care of these customers first, then I'll take care of you." And I said, "I am a customer. My food is out there in the car getting cold." And one of the ladies in line says to the worker, "Well, besides that you're not doing a very good job of taking care of us." And I'm thinking yeah, yeah, here we go. I've never been in a fast food restaurant when the patrons blew it up, so this will be a new experience.

He finally takes care of a few of them; he disappears, comes back, and guess what he's got in his hand? My dollar. And he hands it to me with those wonderful, immortal words, "I'm sorry." And I can't believe I did this—I said, "I know you are. Now apologize." I said, "What is wrong with you? I come in here all the time." I said, "You should have just given me a dollar out of your own pocket.

You could have counted it later and then you could have gotten your dollar back and if you found out I was wrong, it would just cost you a dollar, and as it is you just lost a really good customer. You think I'm ever going to come back here again? On second thought, I'm going to wait a month and then I'm going to come back because I'm pretty sure you won't be here then." I took my dollar and proceeded to the door.

I get out in the car and I sit down and my friend is staring at me. I said, "What?" He says, "What was that?" I said, "What?" He says, "Who are you?" I said, "Okay, that wasn't my best moment. What do you want to do?" He said, "We're going back in."

This is one of the reasons why I try not to have too many spiritual friends. So we go in there. I still don't know what we're going to do. He grabs some napkins and proceeds to start cleaning off tables where people aren't sitting. And I thought, "Okay." So I grab some napkins and I start cleaning tables too. The guy back behind the counter says, "What are you guys doing?" And I said, "Well, it's obvious you're understaffed today, you can't handle the crowd you have here, so what we're going to do is clean up all the tables where people aren't' sitting and then we're going to go on. And by the way, I understand there was a guy who looks a lot like me who was in here earlier. I'm really sorry about that guy."

Everybody has had a moment like that. Please tell me you've had a moment like that. Those are the moments that don't happen when you engage in ninety seconds of prayer through the day. Because they just can't. Those little prayers start to transform life and you keep getting reoriented to where you're going.

Those are two little suggestions about intercessory prayer and praying through the day. My final word is to try these ways of praying and expect God to act. Nothing kills the presence of God like the expectation that he's going to do nothing. I hope you will expect things to happen, lives to be transformed, new vision to be cast, relationships to be healed, and lives to be changed. Be open and inviting. I don't know what God's going to do. But I can promise you it won't be boring.

When Life Becomes Prayer

This brings me to the fifth way of praying, the one that's not in the Thibodeaux book. The fifth way of praying is when all of life becomes prayer—where you take the experience that you've had in listening and talking to God and being with God and you live out that reality in everyday ways.

Maybe the easiest way for me to explain this is to tell you about another experience. When I was at Syracuse University doing graduate work, I had to take a course in non-Western religion. I didn't want to do that because I wasn't interested. So I did what any student would do. I just took the course that worked into my schedule best, and in this case that course was on Mahayana Buddhism. Those of you who know a little about world religions will know there are different kinds of Buddhism. There's Theravada Buddhism, which we associate with India, there's Mahayana Buddhism, which we generally associate with Japan. But to make a long story short, when you think of Mahayana Buddhism, if you think about Zen you'll have it about right.

So here I am sitting in this course on Zen Buddhism and I don't get it. I'm there with all those Buddhologists and they would say, "Open your book to Lotus Sutra such and such," and I couldn't even find it. That was when I really appreciated how my students felt who didn't know who the Galatians were. One of the books we read in the course was called *How to Raise an Ox*. I didn't have an ox, and it didn't look like oxen were going to be a big part of my future.

I remember the day when I went over the edge. We were discussing that most important of all Zen koans (like riddles), which is, "What is the sound of one hand clapping?" And guess what the answer is? The question didn't bother me. I'm a theologian. I'm used to that question. The answer is "love." The sound of one hand clapping is love. And sitting there I said, "Just shoot me. The sound of one hand clapping is not love. I don't know what it is, but it is not love."

So I go to the teacher and I say, "I'm having a little problem here. I don't get it. Now make sure you understand this. It's not the details I'm not getting. I don't get IT. You know, every time I try to grab hold of the IT, it disappears. There's got to be another way to do this." And he says, "Sure. There's a Buddhist monastery up in the mountains. Why don't you go up there and do the immersion thing for a while. See how that works for you." And I said, "I am out of here," and off I went. I get up to the Buddhist monastery and this inscrutable Asian gentleman meets me. I learned to do Zen meditation. I learned to get into the lotus position—and out. That's very important. If you're going to do the Lotus position, you have to have an exit strategy. And if you're wondering, the answer is no. I can no longer get in the lotus position.

I learned to do Zen meditation, really learned to appreciate it, and after I'd been there for a while, I got the opportunity to ask the monk, the Roshi, a question. You don't get to ask very many questions, but I got to ask a question. I had been thinking about it and had prepared my question very carefully. He says, "Mr. Harris, what is your question?" I said, "This is my question. Is it possible to do snow-shoveling Zen?" He pauses for like thirty minutes. They don't get in a hurry there. And he says, "What does this mean, 'Snow-shoveling Zen'?" I thought, "This is great. I'm getting to ask another question." I said, "Well, we're here in upstate New York, we got snow up to our hips, if we could learn to meditate while we shoveled snow, we would not only have a rich interior life, we would have clean sidewalks." I thought this was brilliant.

And so he pauses for like another thirty minutes. Finally, he says to me, "Mr. Harris must first learn to do sitting Zen, then perhaps you can learn to do snow-shoveling Zen." Which made it worth the price of the trip.

You see, I really believe this. I believe snow-shoveling prayer is the deepest, most profound prayer. Let me say it another way. I do not believe prayer exists in heaven. I believe that we will be so overwhelmed by the presence of God in the face of Christ that turning intentionally to that will make no sense. We'll just be there all the time. And if in our lives we could so consistently practice God's presence that he was that close to us all the time, prayer would become totally irrelevant. But, before we can learn to do snow shoveling prayer, we must first learn to do sitting prayer.

So the reason we do these first four kinds of prayer is to lead us to a life that is lived in God's presence more deeply and more consistently, and that's the most profound way to pray. One of the ways that you will judge this is to ask, "Do you see people who live out more consistently the righteousness of God?" It's not going to be about whether people pray more. Rather, it's going to be what lives they live. Is God constantly in their view and in their thinking? Is that what happens?

I think that must be what Paul means when he talks about praying without ceasing. And so we do all of these other kinds of prayer in order to lead us to this life of prayer.

Daily Incompetence

So let me make a few suggestions as to how we can experience God's presence every moment of our day so that life becomes prayer. What I'm going to give you is what's come to be called the Harris Mantra. That is, these are the four things I say to myself first thing in the morning to try to experience the presence of God. Actually these are things two through five. The first thing I say to myself in the morning as I look in the mirror is "Yuck." But that one's not theological. So after I get past that, this is what I say to try to experience the presence of God, and you can take this for what it's worth.

Number one: today I will be incompetent. This one is very important because if you fail on the other three, you have this one to fall back on. It is also important because there is nothing that drives away a sense of the presence of God like the illusion of our own competence. We experience the presence of God when we experience the fact that we are spiritually incompetent in our lives.

Different kinds of teachers attract different kinds of students. I attract a lot of flaky ones. Imagine that. I also attract searchers to my classes. And I know why I get those. I pray for them. I've been praying all summer. If there are students coming to Abilene Christian University who are really struggling with their faith, I want them in my class. Because I struggle with my faith every day and if they care enough to struggle with it, I want to walk with them.

This isn't my point, but I want to say this as strongly as I can. The opposite of faith is not doubt. The opposite of faith is complacency. You give me somebody who cares enough to doubt and we have a good chance. Those students will often wind up in my office at some point or another and we'll be having one of those heaven and hell discussions. This is not a discussion about where they're going to church; this is a discussion about whether they can believe that Jesus Christ is the Son of God. This is a discussion about whether they can invest themselves in any of it or not.

When I'm having that discussion, you know who I feel sitting right here? Their parents. I know there's somebody back home who cares more about this kid than they care about life itself. Those parents are gathered in the room with us. And I have to tell you, it's at those moments when I feel as if I am absolutely incompetent. I don't have the right button to push and I don't have the right lever to pull. If God's Holy Spirit doesn't come into that situation, we are in big trouble. And that's when I say, "God, I know I'm over my head here, come on, come on, come on Holy Spirit." And I tell you, I like that feeling.

When I ministered with the Donalson Church, our elders increasingly became pastoral people; and as they became men of prayer and as they became more and more pastoral, our people brought more and more stuff for them to pray over. We found out we had stuff going on in our church we preferred not to know. Our first reaction was that we were sorry we ever got into this. We were a lot happier when we vaguely knew some stuff was going on, but didn't know what it was.

One of our elders and his wife had been hit with one of these impossible problems by a young couple. The elder's wife came to me afterwards and she cornered me, gripped me by the shirt, shook her finger in my face, and with tears in her eyes says, "I hope you know how incompetent we feel to do this." And I grabbed her hands and I said, "I hope you know how incompetent you are to do this. And that doesn't make you different from anybody. We're all struggling with that. Because that's where we start." Prayer and the presence of God grow out of our understanding that we are incompetent to deal with all that comes our way.

Daily Presence

Number two: today I will be fully present to the people in front of me and to God. I want you to think about this a bit. One of the greatest gifts you can give to another person is to be really present to him or her when you are together. I don't know if you've noticed, but people almost never experience that. You almost never have a person's full and undivided attention in front of you. Part of it is a technology problem. I have my cell phone with me as most of you do. The cell phone is a wonderful servant, but a terrible master.

I was out one time with a guy having a very serious lunch dis-cussion and his cell phone rang three times in the first ten minutes.

He answered it all three times. Finally, I got so frustrated I took my cell phone out, turned it on, and called him. And I said, "It's obvious everybody who calls you gets more attention than I do. I just thought I'd give you a call and see if we could talk." And he turned off his phone, I turned off my mine, and we had a good talk.

But it's not just a matter of technology. It's also that when we're with people we're thinking about what's coming next and we never really become present to them. I implore you to go back and look at the ministry of Jesus; one of the things you will see is that Jesus has encounters with people that often last five or ten minutes, yet to him they are the only people who exist in the world. He's that centered on them. Boy, that's a great gift to give to another person! Those of you who have been engaged in ministry for a while know this great truth—that often the greatest ministry you do is while you're on your way to do what you think is the important ministry.

At the end of every year we take our Bible majors out to the woods to have what we call "senior blessing." It's where we try to help them go from being our students to being our colleagues in ministry. It's a great day and we all have an opportunity to share things with each other. One of the interesting things is when the students share what has been the most meaningful experience of their student career. Almost always that experience was not in class but in a chance conversation with a teacher or fellow student. Those opportunities are there if we are just paying attention to what is in front of us.

One of the deep, dark secrets of my life is that, even though I'm a theologian and a philosopher, what I really like to do is read novels. I subscribe to the *New York Times Book Review* and I'm always looking for off-beat novels. One that caught my eye was one by a great American author, Calvin Trillin. The name of the book was *Tepper Isn't Going Out*. The description of the book hooked me. What Tepper likes to do is drive around New York City trying to find the perfect parking place. And whenever he finds a good parking place, he will park there for as long as it's legal. Inevitably, someone will see him in the car, want the space, and ask, "Are you coming out of that space." And the answer is, "Tepper isn't going out."

A newspaper man finds out about this and writes a story about Tepper and his hobby. Other New Yorkers begin to wonder, "What does he know that we don't?" And so they start looking for him. Whenever they see him someone will come up and knock on his window and say, "Can I come in there and sit with you?" And pretty soon people are lined up outside his car waiting for the opportunity to sit with him. When they say, "Can I come in there and sit with you," Tepper always says the same thing. He says, "Why not?" They then climb into his car and proceed to tell him all of their life's problems. But he never says anything more profound than "Yeah, there is always something." And they feel incredibly helped! They are helped simply because of what he does for the few minutes they're in his car with him. He's just there. He's paying attention.

Okay, but we're Christians. So it's not just a matter of being fully present to the people in front of us. It's also about being fully present to God. That is, it's thinking about what God is trying to do in this situation. In a world as hurting and wounded and broken as ours, every moment is filled with God possibilities. We're just not watching.

Every spring break at my university, we send out student evangelism teams. We have the Los Angeles team, the Hawaii team, and then we have the group I work with. It's called "Seek and Follow." Notice the difference. Seek and Follow is the group that does not know where they're going to go. They don't have a strategic plan. In fact, they have no plan at all. They just pray and then they go. It gets a little flaky sometimes. They'll be driving along, get to a crossroads, and won't know what to do. They'll pray over a map and one of the students says, "I think we should go this way," and off they go. They literally don't know where they're going that week.

Our administration has never liked this campaign. Parents call up in the middle of the week and say, "Where are our children?" and all we can say is, "Only God knows." The students return from their trip and can't wait to report to me: "You aren't going to believe what happened! We went to this place and they needed this done and we had just enough people to do it and then we went to the next place and it happened again and it just kept happening over and over and we know God was leading us all the way."

I believe that. I really do. I tell the students, "I don't think God was leading you the way you think he was, but your hearts were right. You were only asking one thing, and that is, 'What can we do to serve God?' and I believe you could have driven any number of miles in any direction and any place you wound up would have been where God wanted you. And if I'm right, the rest of your life could be a spring break campaign."

This is the key. Today I will be fully present to the people in front of me and to God. How different some disastrous meetings would have been if, before I had gone in, I had been asking God, "What is it you want to happen for the other person?" Because I was so driven by my own agenda and my own notions about what needed to take place, if God had wanted to do something through me, he never had a crack at it. Today I will be fully present to the people in front of me and to God.

Daily Being Christ

Number three: today I will be the Christ. Paul says it this way, "For me to live is Christ and to die is gain." Today I'm going to try to live out the life of Jesus in front of the people I meet. My first job is to show my students what an eccentric, single, bearded theologian at Abilene Christian University would look like if Jesus came in that guise. And their job is to show me what Jesus would look like as a nineteen-year-old. I tell them they have a really important job because the only insight I have into Jesus the teenager is by watching them. I wonder about it a lot. I mean, you parents, can you imagine that you have this teenage kid who not only thinks he's God, but is. We have different kinds of ministry, but our fundamental task is exactly the same: to show what Jesus would look like if he were in our particular circumstance.

When I occasionally have a conflict with a student, and it doesn't happen very often, this is always where we start. We come into my office and I say, "Okay, here's our goal. You need to help me understand how Jesus would treat you if he were sitting where I'm sitting. And I'm going to try to help you understand what Jesus would do if he were in your position here."

One time my parents sent me a newspaper article that meant a lot to me. It described a preacher who was dying of Lou Gehrig's disease. He was preaching in Branson, Missouri, from a wheelchair. The paper said, "For years he's been showing us how to live as a Christian, now he's showing us how you die as a Christian." And I thought, "What a wonderful ministry! Your body has betrayed you and you're in this decline of life and you can still say, 'For me to live is Christ.'" He shows us what Jesus would look like if he were dying with a terminal disease.

Daily Seeing Christ

Number four: today I will see the Christ. I have a good passage on this one. It's a passage that means a lot to me because it got me out of a really tough spot once. I have these rules by which I live my life. I call them canons of life and I have hundreds of them. Some of them are really important and some of them are not so important. One really important one is, "Don't tell God what to do. It annoys him." That's an important one. "Never play chess with someone from an Eastern European country." Andre the Romanian taught me that one. We used to play chess. He would just slaughter me. Then when we'd set the board back up where I was hopelessly hemmed in, he would take my side of the board, and beat me again. I learned a new one not long ago: "Never move a really large houseplant in a room with a ceiling fan."

But on the more important side is this one: "Don't go speak at a place where they don't want you because that makes my life more difficult and theirs." But one time when I was still living in Tennessee I wound up at a place I didn't have any business being. They invited me to come. It didn't exactly seem like a match. I didn't think they really wanted me. I tried to talk them out of it and they said, "No, we want you." And I said, "Have you read my writings?" And they said, "Yes. In fact that's what we want you to come and talk about." And I said, "Okay, is your church all together on this?" And they said, "No. But our leadership is and we want you to come and help move our church where our leadership is." And I said, "That sounds like great work," and so I went to do it.

But they lied to me. Their leadership was split right down the middle. And this was just horrible. I didn't serve this church well and the whole thing was ungodly. They even had a question and answer session set up. So in the question and answer session one old brother was just so frustrated with me he could hardly stand it, and who could blame him. He thought that I didn't think that enough people were going to hell. So finally in his frustration he says, "Do you think anybody's going to hell?" My first reaction was to say, "Well, maybe one." But that would have been ungracious. So I said, "Yes, I think some people are going to hell. In fact, I want to give you a list."

And I started to read the following passage: "I was thirsty and you gave me nothing to drink. I was a stranger and you did not invite me in. I needed clothes and you did not clothe me. I was sick and in prison and you did not look after me." They also answered, "Lord, when did we see you hungry or thirsty or a stranger needing clothes or sick or in prison and did not help you?" He replied, "I tell you the truth. Whatever you did not do for one of the least of these you did not do for me. Then they will go away to eternal punishment and the righteous to eternal life." That's the end of Matthew 25, of course. I said, "Okay, there's my list. Where's yours?"

That's not the only passage on judgment in Scripture. Let's be fair. But it is an interesting one. I assume that that passage is intended to roll back the screen so we can see things as they really are. And what Jesus says here is, "When you see those needy, helpless, maybe sinful people, here is what you should see. You should see me." That makes a huge difference in the way you are in the world, especially if you're not a real people person.

Okay, I'm not very good with people. How many of you have had the Myers Briggs personality profile? That's one of those personality tests that reduces your whole personality to four letters. I am an INTJ. INTJ's are the rarest combination. And you don't have to know all about it. An "I" means an introvert. An "N" is a person who is intuitive. He likes ideas. "T" is a thinker as opposed to a feeler, and the last one has to do with whether you like to get your ducks in a row. I'm a weak "J" so I like to get my ducks in a row, but they keep wandering off.

So here I am. I'm this introverted, thinking, intuitive guy. I can tell you two quick things and you'll understand INTJ. If you say to an INTJ we are going to lock you in the library alone and you are not going to be able to get out, we say, "Bring it on." The thing with an INTJ is, if I'm going to serve people, it's never going to be because of my continuing admiration for them. Because I don't find them very admirable. But you serve people because when you see that person what you see is Jesus Christ. You may get tired of people, but when you're a Christian, you don't get tired of Jesus.

Tonight at midnight you may decide to spend the night in a Benedictine monastery. So you go and you pound on their door at midnight and say, "Let me in." You know what they will do? They will say, "Come on in." Because they are afraid if they turn you away that you are going to turn out to be Jesus. Don't you hate it when that happens?

Honesty requires me to tell you that this is the biggest struggle in my life right now. Over the last fifteen years I have had a wonderful ministry to people preparing for ministry and a wonderful ministry to searchers. I have had little ministry to those who are indifferent or hostile to the gospel on my campus. And I've started praying to God to change that. I want to come to love them and get into their world and see what happens. And I don't know how to do that. The way I've started doing it is this: at 11:00 PM every Thursday night I go to one of the dorms to play cards. Not 11:00 AM., 11:00 PM, because there are some kids who will play cards with me who won't take my classes or come to my office to talk to me about their spiritual life. The first goal is just to love them. You should have seen their faces when I got an ace on the river to win my first hand of Texas Hold 'Em. I told them that's what happens when you play poker with someone God loves. I think that we need to find ways to see Jesus in every one we see. And boy, does that change the way you are in the world!

Okay, here we are. Today I will be incompetent. Today I will be fully present to the people in front of me and to God. Today I will be the Christ. Today I will see the Christ. This may seem to be an unusual lesson in a chapter on prayer, but I feel strongly that what we do in prayer has to become part of the bigger fabric of our lives. You can't have your prayer life over here and then the rest of life just going on its own way. Every moment has to become a time of practicing God's presence.

We engage in these times of brief but intense sitting prayer so that when we're in the trenches with people, we'll be fully aware of God's presence there. And it's hard to get there without committing yourself to the life of prayer. I want to make sure we have the goals straight. The goal is not to have us praying more. The goal is to have us aware of and practicing God's presence every moment of every day. It's then God will be all in all.

CONCLUSION

The Christian mystics don't agree on much, but they all agree on what lies at the end of the journey: the discovery that God is love. To be embraced in the relentless love of God changes everything. To *know* that there is nothing you could ever do to make God love you more is the single most transformative truth in the world. It empowers you to pray in wholly new ways.

In conclusion, let me share with you what I believe to be the most powerful and dangerous prayer you can pray—the Wesleyan Covenant prayer:

I am no longer my own, but yours.
Put me to what you will, rank me with whom you will;
Put me to doing, put me to suffering.
Let me be employed for you or laid aside by you.
Let me be full, let me be empty.
Let me have all things, let me have nothing.
I freely and heartily yield all things
    to your pleasure and disposal.
And now, O glorious and blessed God,
Father, Son, and Holy Spirit,
You are mine, and I am yours. So be it.
And the covenant which I have made on earth,
    let it be ratified in heaven.
Amen.

One cannot dare to pray this unless you believe in the core of your being that, however God responds to this prayer, the response will be one of eternal love.

It is five in the morning. I have that ache in my heart that is such a familiar companion. The longing for the time when we no longer see through a glass darkly, but face to face. The time when words such as these are no longer necessary. The time when we know first-hand what Jesus knows about the loving Father. Whittier, one more time:

> O Sabbath rest by Galilee!
> O calm of hills above,
> Where Jesus knelt to share with Thee
> The silence of eternity
> Interpreted by love!
>
> Come Lord Jesus!